THE QUOTABLE JOE

CORN POP, DOG-FACED PONY
SOLDIERS, AND OTHER MALARKEY
FROM AMERICA'S MOST
EMBARRASSING CANDIDATE

KATHERINE RODRIGUEZ

BOMBARDIER
BOOKS

A BOMBARDIER BOOKS BOOK
An Imprint of Post Hill Press
ISBN: 978-1-64293-798-5
ISBN (eBook): 978-1-64293-799-2

The Quotable Joe:
Corn Pop, Dog-Faced Pony Soldiers, and Other Malarkey from
America's Most Embarrassing Candidate
© 2020 by Katherine Rodriguez
All Rights Reserved

Cover Design by Cody Corcoran
Joe Biden photo by Gage Skidmore

Post Hill Press
New York • Nashville
posthillpress.com

Published in the United States of America

CONTENTS

INTRODUCTION

Joe Biden has gotten away with saying some of the zaniest things throughout his career as a politician spanning thirty-six years in the Senate and eight years as former president Barack Obama's vice president. He also mounted unsuccessful bids for the presidency in 1988 and 2008, each time saying some of the most darndest things in political history and current events. As "Sleepy Joe" prepares to head into the general election season, he's said a lot of things that he will have to explain on the campaign trail to voters. Some of the things he will have to explain to his voters are his racist and sexist comments, lies and flip-flops, made-up stories, awkward questions, and just plain puzzling and head-scratching moments. I've written this book as a curation of some of Biden's zaniest quotes so you, the reader, can decide for yourself how to judge Biden as a candidate this 2020 election season.

CHAPTER 1

RACIAL AND SEXUAL MALAPROPISMS

B iden has a lot to answer for in his comments on race and sex throughout his lifetime. As Biden prepares to head into the general election, voters will want to know about his history, from his racist comments in the 1970s to his sexist comments more recently in the #MeToo movement.[1] Biden has faced criticism over many positions in his life as a public servant and in his private life, including his handling of Anita Hill's testimony during then-Supreme Court nominee Clarence Thomas's nomination hearing in 1991, which will be discussed later in this book.

Joe Biden Was Once Concerned about the Civil Rights Movement

"During the 60's, I was, in fact, very concerned about the civil rights movement," he said. But at another point he said, "I was not an activist," adding:

> I worked at an all-black swimming pool in the east side of Wilmington, Delaware. I was involved in what they were thinking, what they

were feeling. But I was not out marching. I was not down in [sic] not out marching. I was not down in Selma. I was not anywhere else. I was a suburbanite kid who got a dose of exposure to what was happening to black Americans.

"When I was 17, I participated in sit-ins to desegregate restaurants and movie houses," he declared then. "And my stomach turned upon hearing the voices of Faubus and Wallace. My soul raged on seeing Bull Connor and his dogs."

The senator's press secretary at the time, Larry Rasky, tried to clear up some of the confusion when he said that when he was younger in Wilmington, Biden "did participate in action to desegregate one restaurant and one movie theater."[2]

Joe Biden Once Used "Roaches" to Describe Black Kids

Biden was sharing a personal story about his days in his youth working as a lifeguard at the community pool in Wilmington, where there were a lot of black kids.

"By the way, you know, I sit on the stand, and it get[s] hot. I got a lot, I got hairy legs that, that, that, that turn blonde in the sun, and the kids used to come up and reach in the pool and rub my leg down so it was straight and then watch the hair come back up again. They'd look at it. I learned about roaches, I learned about kids jumping on my lap," Biden said.[3]

Biden's use of the word "roaches" was used without any context when talking about his time as a lifeguard.

Biden: Japanese Women Are Only Employed Because of "Xenophobia"

Biden suggested that Japanese women are only employed because of "xenophobia" while out on the campaign trail in Spartanburg, South Carolina, in August 2019.[4]

"Japan is in a position where traditionally women are as well-educated as men, but the tradition was, once they had a child, they were to drop out of the job market," Biden said.

The former vice president then claimed that Japan was only encouraging women to stay in the job market to prevent the need to import foreign workers into the country.

"There's an entire move, because they're xenophobic—because they don't want to invite other people from outside their country to come in and make up the workforce—they have fewer workers than they have a need for workers," Biden said. "And so, what they've done is they've decided to encourage women to stay in the job market."

Joe Biden Once Advocated Segregation in 1975, Claiming "Black Pride"

Biden, who is weighing a 2020 presidential bid, once advocated school segregation in the U.S. back in 1975, arguing that it benefited minority groups and allowed them to embrace "their own identity."

He opposed the federally mandated "busing" policy that was designed to stop school segregation. Over the past few decades, he has claimed he wanted desegregation but disagreed on the policy of busing.

"I think the concept of busing...that we are going to integrate people so that they all have the same access and they learn to grow up with one another and all the rest, is a rejection of the whole movement of black pride," said Biden.[5] Desegregation, he argued, was "a rejection of the entire black awareness concept, where black is beautiful, black culture should be studied; and the cultural awareness of the importance of their own identity, their own individuality."

When Biden ran for the Senate in 1972, he supported busing white kids to inner city schools and black kids to the suburbs. But that changed once he got elected to the Senate. In 1974, Biden's white constituents started an anti-busing lobby. White parents demanded answers from Biden to see what he was going to do to keep their kids from being reassigned to majority-black schools.

In 1977, Biden still took an anti-busing stance, albeit with a more personal plea for "orderly integration."

"Unless we do something about this, my children are going to grow up in a jungle, the jungle being a racial jungle with tensions having built so high that it is going to explode at some point," Biden said shortly after making a plea for "orderly integration."[6] "We have got to make some move on this."

African Americans made up 14.3 percent of Delaware's population in 1970, U.S. Census Bureau data shows.[7] White voters in the state, whom Biden depended on to be reelected in 1978, overwhelmingly opposed busing.

It paid off for Biden, because he was overwhelmingly reelected by 16 percent of the vote in 1978.

Later in his career, Biden said he questioned "the blacks on staff" whether he had something "in me that's deep-seated that I don't know."

And in 2008, after then-Democratic presidential candidate Barack Obama chose Biden as his running mate, Biden said, "The struggle for civil rights was the animating political element of my life."

Biden's conclusion on busing was not arrived at lightly.

"I give you my word as a Biden, I put in over 100 hours, by far—I would say close to 300 hours—on just torturing this [anti-busing concept]. Calling my staff together, and the blacks on my staff together, saying 'Look, this is what I think. Do you think I am [racist]? Is there something in me that's deep-seated that I don't know?'"[8]

Joe Biden Once Worked with Segregationist Senators

Biden faced calls from fellow Democrats to apologize for his nostalgic history of working with segregationist Democratic senators in the 1970s and the 1980s.

"I was in a caucus with James O. Eastland. He never called me 'boy,' he always called me 'son,'" Biden told donors at a New York fundraiser.[9]

"Well, guess what? At least there was some civility. We got things done. We didn't agree on much of anything. We got things done. We got it finished. But today, you look at the other side and you're the enemy. Not the opposition, the enemy. We don't talk to each other anymore."

Sen. Cory Booker (D-NJ) was one of those to demand an apology, but Biden refused to apologize and said that he should instead apologize to him for verbally attacking him.

Joe Biden Once Voted to Restore U.S. Citizenship to Confederate President Jefferson Davis

Biden voted to honor Confederate leaders now scorned by his fellow Democrats and the Black Lives Matter movement as racists and traitors who need to be expelled from history.[10] He joined a unanimous Senate in voting for Robert E. Lee's citizenship in 1975, and he voted for Jefferson Davis's citizenship in 1977. Former president Jimmy Carter signed the latter bill granting Davis citizenship into law in 1977.

Joe Biden Once Praised Segregationist Senators...Twice!

In 1988, on the floor of the U.S. Senate, Biden praised segregationist Sen. John Stennis (D-MS) as a "man of character" even after the Democrat opposed *Brown v. Board of Education* with the Southern Manifesto.

"And to think that I would be one day on the floor of the United States Senate, being paid such accolades by such a man of character and courage as Sen. John Stennis, is beyond any such expectation of my wildest dreams, and I mean that sincerely," Biden said.[11]

Biden has even bragged about being gifted the table that the Southern Manifesto was signed on.[12]

He also paid homage more recently to a late reformed segregationist senator, the late Sen. Fritz Hollings (D-SC), at a September 2019 fundraiser.

"Folks, I'm going to be brief because you're standing and because old Fritz will come down from heaven and yank my neck back," Biden told donors, according to the *Post and Courier*.[13] "By the way, I owe South Carolina more than you can imagine."

Hollings once opposed integration and opposed the *Brown v. Board of Education* decision, using it as his platform when he ran for governor of South Carolina. He eventually changed his position and supported integration.[14]

"Good for the Negro"

Biden was asked at a 1973 speech he gave at the City Club in Cleveland, Ohio, fresh off his election to the Senate, whether he had spoken with his Southern colleagues about how they felt about "the problems of the Negro in America."

"I think the two-party system, although my Democratic colleagues won't like me saying this, is good for the South and good for the Negro, good for the black in the South," Biden responded.[15] "Other than the fact that [the Southern senators] still call me boy, I think they've changed their mind a little bit."

"Mainstream African American"

In 2007, when Biden was on a conference call with reporters, he talked about the strengths of then-presidential candidate Barack Obama.

"I mean you've got the first sort of mainstream African American, who is articulate and bright, and clean and [a] nice-looking guy. I mean, that's a storybook, man," Biden said.[16]

Biden later apologized for his statement, but Obama later issued a written statement calling his comments "historically inaccurate."

"I didn't take Sen. Biden's comments personally, but obviously they were historically inaccurate. African-American presidential candidates like Jesse Jackson, Shirley Chisholm, Carol Moseley Braun and Al Sharpton gave a voice to many important issues through their campaigns, and no one would call them inarticulate," Obama said.[17]

Biden Referred to Asia as "the Orient"

When Biden was vice president back in 2014, he gave a speech in Iowa and referred to parts of Asia as "the Orient" just hours after apologizing for a separate gaffe.

"You know on the way back from Mumbai to go meet with President Xi [Jinping] in China, I stopped in Singapore to meet with a guy named Lee Kuan Yew, who most foreign policy experts around the world say is the wisest man in the Orient," Biden said.[18]

The term "orient" is considered to be an offensive way to describe Asia as a continent.

"Shylocks"

Then-vice president Biden was giving a speech to the Legal Services Corporation while telling a story about his son, Beau, who provided legal assistance to soldiers after they came home from war.

"People would come to him and talk about what was happening to them at home in terms of foreclosures, in terms of bad loans that were being—I mean, these shylocks who took advantage of these women and men while overseas," Biden said.[19]

The term "shylock," which refers to the Jewish villain in Shakespeare's *Merchant of Venice*, has anti-Semitic connotations. Abraham Foxman, the head of the Anti-Defamation League, said Biden "should have been more careful" with his words.

Biden later apologized.

Indian Accents in Delaware

In 2006, Biden made a racist co
tion of Indian Americans in De
   "You cannot go to a 7-Ele
you have a slight Indian accent.

"Poor Kids Are Just as Br

Biden told a group of majority Asian and
August 2019 at the Asian and Latino Coalition in Des Moines,
Iowa, while campaigning for the 2020 primary elections that
"poor kids are just as bright" as white kids.[21]

   "We should challenge students in these schools and have
advanced placement programs in these schools," Biden said.
"We have this notion that somehow if you're poor, you cannot
do it. Poor kids are just as bright, just as talented, as white kids."
He quickly added, "Wealthy kids, black kids, Asian kids, no I
really mean it, but think how we think about it."

"Put Y'all Back in Chains"

When Biden was stumping on the 2012 campaign trail, he was
discussing 2012 Republican candidate Mitt Romney's plan for
Wall Street, telling an audience that included many African
Americans, "They're going to put y'all back in chains."[22]

   He received a lot of blowback from the Romney campaign.
The Obama campaign called the controversy "faux outrage," but
they also had to release a statement clarifying that Biden's comments were a reference to Republican remarks about unchaining
the private sector and his unshackling of the middle class, CBS
News reported.[23]

...e First Black Woman to the Senate"

...iving a campaign speech in Sumter, South Carolina,
...forgot that there were already two black women serv-
...i Congress's upper chamber.

"I'm looking forward to appointing the first African American woman to the United States Senate," Biden said in his stump speech.[24]

Biden forgot that Carol Moseley Braun (D-IL) served as the first black female senator from 1993 to 1999, while Sen. Kamala Harris (D-CA) was the second black woman to be elected to the Senate beginning in 2017.

"I Came Out of the Black Community"

Biden claimed during the November 2019 Democratic debate that he "came out of the black community."[25]

"I come out of the black community in terms of my support," Biden said, noting that three former chairmen of the Congressional Black Caucus had endorsed his campaign as well as "the only African-American woman who'd ever been elected to the United States Senate."

He was fact-checked in real time that night by Sen. Cory Booker (D-NJ) and Sen. Kamala Harris (D-CA), the second black senator to be elected to the U.S. Senate.

Biden also claimed Barack Obama chose him to be his running mate for president because of his ties "to the black community."

"One of the reasons I was picked to be vice president was because of my relationship, long-standing relationship with the black community," he said. "I was part of that coalition."

But Obama's pick of Biden as a running mate was widely due to his ability to provide outreach to blue-collar voters because of his ties to Scranton, Pennsylvania.[26]

"You Ain't Black" If You Don't Support Me over Trump

Biden declared in an interview with Charlamagne tha God in May 2020 that if black Americans were unsure whether to support Donald Trump over him in the November 2020 election, then "you ain't black."[27]

"If you have a problem figuring out whether you're for me or Trump, then you ain't black," Biden told Charlamagne.

"George Floyd's Death Had More of an Impact on Society Than MLK's Assassination"

Biden said in June 2020 that George Floyd's death in the hands of Minneapolis police officers could have a greater impact on civil rights than Dr. Martin Luther King's 1968 assassination.

"Even Dr. King's assassination did not have the worldwide impact that George Floyd's death did," Biden said.[28] "It's just like television changed the civil rights movement for the better when they saw Bull Connor and his dogs ripping the clothes off of elderly black women going to church and firehoses ripping the skin off of young kids."

Alveda King, King's niece, said Biden was "missing the mark" by comparing the two and that all Biden was doing was "stirring the race card up."[29]

Biden: Trump Supporters Believe "Mexicans Are Rapists," "All Muslims Are Bad"

Biden claimed that some supporters of President Donald Trump believe that "all Mexicans are rapists" and "all Muslims are bad." He made the comments at a virtual fundraiser in April 2020.[30]

"There are people who support the president because they like the fact that he is engaged in political division," Biden told the donors. "They really support the notion that, you know, all Mexicans are rapists and all Muslims are bad and…dividing this nation based on ethnicity, race."

Biden: If People "Believe Tara Reade They Probably Shouldn't Vote for Me"

Biden said during a May 2020 appearance on MSNBC's *The Last Word with Lawrence O'Donnell* that if voters believed Tara Reade, the Senate staffer who accused Biden of sexually assaulting her in 1993, "they probably shouldn't vote for me."[31]

Biden said:

> I think they should vote their heart, and if they believe Tara Reade, they probably shouldn't vote for me. I wouldn't vote for me if I believed Tara Reade. The fact is that, look at Tara Reade's story. It changes considerably. And so—but, I don't want to question her motive. I don't want to question anything, other than to say, the truth matters. This is being vetted. It's been vetted. They went, and people interviewed scores of my employees over my whole career. This is just totally, thoroughly, completely out of char-

acter, and the idea that in a public place, in a hallway, I would assault a woman… I promise you, it never happened. It should be vetted. She should be thoroughly looked at, and whether or not these happened, look at the story, follow the storyline, and determine whether there's any truth to it, and there is no truth to it. I promise you.

Reade alleged that in 1993, Biden forced his fingers inside her in a Senate hallway. She filed a complaint with the Washington, D.C., Metro Police Department.

Biden told O'Donnell that he didn't remember Reade.

Biden's Lucy Flores Problem

Although it is not a Biden quote, it is a tale of one time Biden allegedly sexually harassed a woman while stumping for her on the campaign trail. Lucy Flores, a former Democratic lieutenant governor nominee in Nevada, was one of the women Biden allegedly sexually harassed. She wrote in a March 2019 essay in *New York Magazine*'s "The Cut" about her experience with the former vice president:[32]

As I was taking deep breaths and preparing myself to make my case to the crowd, I felt two hands on my shoulders. I froze. "Why is the vice-president of the United States touching me?"

I felt him get closer to me from behind. He leaned further in and inhaled my hair. I was mortified. I thought to myself, "I didn't wash

my hair today and the vice-president of the
United States is smelling it. And also, what in
the actual fuck? Why is the vice-president of
the United States smelling my hair?" He proceeded to plant a big slow kiss on the back of
my head. My brain couldn't process what was
happening. I was embarrassed. I was shocked. I
was confused. There is a Spanish saying, "*trag-
ame tierra*," it means, "earth, swallow me whole."
I couldn't move and I couldn't say anything. I
wanted nothing more than to get Biden away
from me. My name was called and I was never
happier to get on stage in front of an audience.

Biden's Touching Jokes Spark Complaints

Biden was making his first public appearance since getting complaints from multiple women about inappropriate touching that
made them feel uncomfortable.

Biden took the stage in Washington, D.C., at an
International Brotherhood of Electrical Workers union gath-
ering in April 2019 when the president of the union, Lonnie
Stephenson, introduced him.

"I just want you to know—I had permission to hug Lonnie,"
Biden replied.[33] The mostly male crowd roared with laughter.

Later on in the gathering, he made a similar joke after invit-
ing a bunch of children on stage and placing his arm around a
young boy.

"By the way, he gave me permission to touch him," the former vice president said, again to laughter.

"Everybody knows I like kids more than people," Biden said.

After Biden's joke, Lucy Flores went on Fox News and called the whole appearance "so incredibly disrespectful."[34]

"The basis of the behavior that I talked about was something much more serious than just a hug," Flores said.

"She Pulled *Me* Close"

Biden continued to make a punchline out of allegations that he inappropriately touched women and got too involved in their personal space.

"I want the press to know, she pulled me close," Biden told attendees at a June 2019 town hall event in Berlin, New Hampshire, referring to a woman at the event who whispered in his ear after she handed him a chair.[35]

Biden: Trump Is America's First "Racist" President

Biden said Trump was America's first "racist" president during a late July virtual town hall organized by the Service Employees International Union (SEIU).[36] He was responding to a healthcare worker who was concerned that Trump was blaming Asians for the coronavirus pandemic.

"No sitting president has ever done this," Biden said.[37] "Never, never, never. No Republican president has done this. No Democratic president. We've had racists, and they've existed, they've tried to get elected president. He's the first one that has."

"And the way he pits people against one another is all designed to divide the country, divide people, not pull them together," Biden continued. "Look what he's doing now. He's blaming everything on China.... He's using it as a wedge."

Despite Biden's claim that Trump is America's first "racist" president, several other presidents before Donald Trump have been avowed racists, such as President Woodrow Wilson, a Democrat who called black people "an ignorant and inferior race."[38]

Biden Quoted Racist Comments When He Used the N-Word in 1985

Although Biden did not make the statement himself, he was quoting a racist statement from a Louisiana state legislator during a redistricting process overseen by a deputy attorney general nominee. Biden was questioning the nominee, William Bradford Reynolds, in 1985 during a Senate Judiciary Committee hearing.[39] Biden used the racist comments to build a case against Reynolds's nomination, asking Reynolds repeatedly if Louisiana was intentionally discriminating against black residents by opposing a majority black district.

"They brought to your attention the allegation that important legislators in defeating the Nunez plan, in the basement, said, 'We already have a n----- mayor, we don't need any more n----- big shots,'" Biden said during the hearing.[40]

CHAPTER 2

LIES AND FLIP-FLOPS

Biden has lied and flip-flopped on so many votes in his Senate career, and his lies and flip-flops have made their way to his speech patterns as well. He once said he was the most qualified person to be president, even though he is a self-described "gaffe machine," and has lied so many times to the public when fumbling over his statements. In this chapter, I will talk about how he first started lying back in law school when he plagiarized a paper and will talk about some of his flip-flop votes on gun control, immigration, the Iraq War, gay marriage, and even Juneteenth. I will also talk about how he flip-flopped on his decision to run in the 2020 election and other falsehoods he has said.

> "I am a gaffe machine, but my God what a wonderful thing compared to a guy who can't tell the truth," he said. "I'm ready to litigate all those things, the question is what kind of nation are we becoming? What are we going to do? Who are we?"[41]

Law School Plagiarism

"It all came out in the wash—I never did plagiarize, I never did—and it all was proven that that never happened," Biden said in 2018 of a law school paper he wrote.[42]

But in a 1987 *New York Times* interview when he was running for president that year, Biden admitted that he plagiarized, acknowledging a "mistake in his youth" but not in a "malevolent" way.

"I was wrong, but I was not malevolent in any way," Biden said.[43] "I did not intentionally move to mislead anybody. And I didn't. To this day I didn't."

Biden, then a 44-year-old Delaware Democrat in charge of the Senate Judiciary Committee, released his transcripts from the Syracuse University College of Law showing poor grades and details of the plagiarism.

The plagiarized article, "Tortious Acts as a Basis for Jurisdiction in Products Liability Cases," was published in the May 1965 edition of the *Fordham Law Review*.[44]

In a letter defending himself in November 1965, Biden begged faculty not to expel him from law school.

"My intent was not to deceive anyone," Biden wrote.[45] "For if it were, I would not have been so blatant."

The faculty ruled he would get an F in the course, but they would strike the grade from his transcript if he retook the course the next year.

He eventually wound up with an 80 percent grade in the course. When Biden graduated from law school in 1968, he was seventy-sixth out of a class of eighty-five.[46]

Biden Lied in 1987 with Claim He Marched in the Civil Rights Movement

Biden was campaigning for the Democratic nomination for the first time in 1987 when he falsely claimed he marched in the civil rights movement.

"When I marched in the civil rights movement, I did not march with a 12-point program," Biden said in New Hampshire in February 1987, according to the *New York Times*.[47] "I marched with tens of thousands of others to change attitudes. And we changed attitudes."

His advisers had to gently remind him that he did not, in fact, march in the civil rights movement, but he kept telling the story anyway.

A few months later in September 1987, Biden's lies and "recklessness as a candidate" caught up with him, and Biden brazenly spoke to reporters at a press conference.

"I've done some dumb things," Biden said at that presser.[48] "And I'll do dumb things again."

Biden Voted for and against the War in Iraq

Biden claimed that despite voting in 2002 to authorize military force against Iraq, he opposed it from "the moment" it started.[49]

But Biden never outright opposed military force in Iraq immediately after the start of the invasion, as he claimed.

During the second Democratic 2020 primary debate on July 31, 2019, Biden said he had "bad judgement" when he voted to authorize former president George W. Bush to use military force in Iraq in 2002 and that he was "trusting the president saying he was only doing this to get inspectors in and get the U.N. to agree to put inspectors in."[50]

Flashback to 2002.

On the day the Iraq War broke out, Biden said, "We voted to give him [Bush] the authority to wage that war. We should step back and be supportive."[51]

During an interview with NPR back in September 2019, he again claimed he spoke out against the war, saying, "Immediately, the moment [shock and awe] started, I came out against the war at that moment."[52]

The Biden campaign also gave a statement to the *Washington Post*, saying, "Vice President Biden misspoke by saying that he declared his opposition to the war immediately."[53]

"He opposed the way we went to war and the way the war was being carried out," the statement continued. "He has for many years called his vote a mistake and takes full responsibility for it. The Bush Administration assured then-Senator Biden that the purpose of the Authorization for the Use of Military Force was to strengthen our position at the U.N. Security Council to get weapons inspectors back into Iraq, and that diplomacy would be exhausted without a premature rush to war."

Biden Once Voted for Strengthening the U.S. Border and against Amnesty for Illegal Aliens

In 2006, Biden sided with Bush for strengthening border security and voting against amnesty for illegal aliens.

"Folks, I voted for a fence, I voted, unlike most Democrats—and some of you won't like it—I voted for 700 miles of fence," he said in 2006.[54]

But in more recent years, Biden has taken the time to call out President Donald Trump for implementing those very same policies as "racist."[55]

Biden Used Term "Undocumented Alien" during March 2020 Democratic Primary Debate

Biden slipped up during the March 2020 Democratic primary debate with CNN, calling the illegal immigrant population "undocumented aliens."[56]

The term "undocumented aliens" is strictly disavowed by the open borders lobby. Biden eventually corrected himself and said "undocumented person."

"There are certain things you cannot deport an undocumented alien for, an undocumented person for," Biden said.[57] "And that would be one of them."

Biden Wronged His Boss on Gay Marriage

In a 2012 episode of *Meet the Press*, Biden wronged the White House by publicly coming out in support of gay marriage. Biden said he was "absolutely comfortable" with the subject, yet he preempted much of what the Obama administration was trying to achieve by slowly and steadily assessing the political risks of fully endorsing gay marriage at the time.

"I am absolutely comfortable with the fact that men marrying men, women marrying women and heterosexual men and women marrying one another are entitled to the same exact rights, all the civil rights, all the civil liberties," Biden said,[58] while noting that then-president Barack Obama, not he, was the person in charge of setting policy on such matters.

Politico reported that the White House was sent scrambling.[59] It pushed then-president Barack Obama to make a judgement call on same-sex marriage sooner than expected.

Biden Did Not Sponsor, Co-Sponsor Juneteenth Bills While He Served as Senator, Now Champions Holiday

Breitbart News reported that former vice president Joe Biden did not sponsor or co-sponsor a single Juneteenth bill while he served as a senator, though now he is attempting to encourage the holiday.[60]

Juneteenth marks the day that slaves in Galveston, Texas, were informed that they were freed on June 19, 1865, by President Abraham Lincoln in the Emancipation Proclamation more than two years prior.

Breitbart did a search of GovTrack congressional records and legislation dating back to 1973, when Biden entered the Senate, to find that he did not co-sponsor or sponsor any of the six bills introduced to make it a holiday:[61]

- 1997
  —S. J. Res. 11 (105th)
  —introduced by Sen. Trent Lott (R-MS),
  two Democrat and two Republican co-sponsors
- 2001
  —S. Con. Res. 51 (107th)
  —introduced by Sen. Sam Brownback (R-KS),
  one Republican co-sponsor
- 2005
  —S. Con. Res. 42 (109th)
  —introduced by Sen. Barack Obama (D-IL),
  two Democrat co-sponsors
- 2006
  —S. Res. 516 (109th)
  —introduced by Sen. Barack Obama (D-IL),
  two Democrat and two Republican co-sponsors

- 2007
  —S. Res. 231 (110th)
  —introduced by Sen. Dick Durbin (D-IL),
  twenty-three co-sponsors (nineteen Democrat,
  two Republican, two Independent)
- 2008
  —S. Res. 584 (110th)
  —introduced by Sen. Dick Durbin (D-IL),
  eighteen co-sponsors (sixteen Democrat,
  one Republican, one Independent)

Despite Biden's Senate history of not sponsoring or co-sponsoring any legislation having to do with the holiday, he wrote in a recent piece in *Essence* in June 2020 that Juneteenth is "a day of profound weight and power."[62]

"The Psalms tell us that 'Weeping may endure for a night, but joy cometh in the morning.' Juneteenth contains both the long, hard night—the two-and-a-half years those enslaved in Galveston, Texas, endured before learning of their emancipation—and the promise of the brighter morning to come," Biden wrote.[63]

Biden Spread Panic about the Swine Flu

In a 2009 interview on NBC's *Today* show, Biden caused panic by telling Americans not to fly or take subways.

"I would tell members of my family—and I have—I wouldn't go anywhere in confined places now," Biden said.[64] "It's not that it's going to Mexico. It's [that] you're in a confined aircraft. When one person sneezes, it goes all the way through the aircraft."

"So, from my perspective, what it relates to is mitigation. If you're out in the middle of a field when someone sneezes, that's one thing. If you're in a closed aircraft or closed container or closed car or closed classroom, it's a different thing," he continued.

The Obama administration had to walk back his statements and issue an apology for creating mass panic for people traveling on airlines and mass transit.

Joe Biden Falsely Claimed He Saved Millions of Lives from Ebola

At the Democratic debate in South Carolina on February 25, 2020, Biden claimed he played a role in saving "millions of lives" throughout the Ebola epidemic that occurred during the Obama administration.[65]

"What we did with Ebola—I was part of making sure that pandemic did not get to the United States, saved millions of lives. And what we did, we set up, I helped set up that office in the presidency, in the president's office, on diseases that are pandemic diseases," Biden said.[66]

"We increased the budget of the CDC. We increased the NIH budget. We should—and our president today—and he's wiped all that out. We did it. We stopped it," he continued.

But according to CDC statistics, the 2014–2016 Ebola epidemic which centered around Africa included 28,600 infections and 11,325 confirmed fatalities.[67]

He also repeatedly referred to Ebola as a "pandemic," which means that a disease has spread globally, instead of an "epidemic," which is more localized.

Joe Biden Falsely Claimed He Created "Shovel-Ready Jobs"

Biden delivered a short speech in late July 2020 in New Castle, Delaware, about child care and elder care benefits (which would be paid for by raising taxes). The former vice president reminded everyone that he had been in charge of the 2009 "stimulus," also known as the American Recovery and Reinvestment Act.

The stimulus was a huge flop and cost the U.S. $862 million on state and local governments and Democrat special interests, but Biden cast his record in a positive light.

"When we usually talk about jobs packages, there's a big push on 'shovel-ready jobs,'" Biden said.[68] "I'm the guy, as you may remember [who] managed the Recovery Act of 800-plus billion dollars. I always focused on 'shovel-ready jobs,' what we could do immediately, to get the money out in communities."

In October 2010, former president Barack Obama admitted that "'there's no such thing as shovel-ready projects' when it comes to public works," the *New York Times* reported.[69]

One year later, Obama cracked a joke at his jobs council, saying, "Shovel-ready wasn't as…uh…shovel-ready as we thought."[70]

Biden Falsely Claimed He Worked on the Paris Climate Deal with a Long Dead Chinese Leader

Biden mistakenly claimed in February 2020 that he worked on the Paris Climate Accord with former Chinese leader Deng Xiaoping, who died more than twenty years before the deal was signed back in 1997.

"One of the things I'm proudest of is getting passed, getting moved, getting in control of the Paris Climate Accord," Biden said in a speech at the College of Charleston.[71] "I'm the guy who came back after meeting with Deng Xiaoping and making the case that I believe China will join if we put pressure on them. We got almost 200 nations to join."

Biden Falsely Claimed His Deceased Son Was the U.S. Attorney General

Biden was delivering remarks at a CNN town hall event where he said his deceased son Beau Biden was attorney general of the United States, a position held by Loretta Lynch and Eric Holder during the Obama administration.[72] Beau Biden served as the attorney general of Delaware.

"My son—my deceased son—was the Attorney General of the United States and before that, he was a federal prosecutor in one of the largest office's [sic] in the country in Philadelphia," Biden said.[73]

Biden Falsely Claimed He Defeated ISIS

Biden falsely claimed in January 2020 that he, along with the rest of the Obama administration, defeated the Islamic State (ISIS).[74] However, the group, which was founded in 1999, did not significantly rise to power until the early 2010s.

"I was part of the coalition that put together 68 counties to deal with stateless terror as well as failed states. Not us alone, 68 other countries, that's how we were able to defeat and end the caliphate [of] ISIS," Biden said of his work during the Obama administration.[75]

Despite Biden's claims, the Obama administration proved to be inefficient at fighting the terror group. It was only after

President Donald Trump took office in 2017 that ISIS began to cede fighters and territory.

Biden Falsely Claimed Billionaire Donors Have Opposed Everything He's Ever Done

Biden was debating his 2020 primary opponents in December 2019, especially taking a dig at Sen. Bernie Sanders, who suggested that he was part of the billionaire class.

"The idea that [Bernie Sanders] is suggesting that I am in the pocket of billionaires when in fact they oppose everything I've ever done and continue to do," Biden said during the PBS/Politico Debate.[76]

In reality, forty-four billionaires and counting are backing Biden's campaign, including Hewlett-Packard CEO Meg Whitman and ex-Google CEO Eric Schmidt.[77]

Biden Claimed He Turned Out Just as Many Black Voters as Obama Did in 2008 and in 2012

Biden suggested during a December 2019 interview with Politico in Iowa that he was responsible for turning out just as many black voters as then-president Barack Obama did in the 2008 and 2012 elections.[78] He also said he did not need Obama's endorsement to win the demographic.

"I was the one who was sent in," he said.[79] "And the reason was, because all the polling and data showed that I had those relationships with the base of the Democratic Party as well as African-Americans. And so I did as many African Americans events as Barack did."

Although it is difficult to gauge how much turnout Biden spurred given that he and Obama were on the same ticket,

Biden sought out black voters but got tripped up by his history of working with segregationist senators to oppose busing.

Anita Hill

Biden said he took "responsibility" for the way Anita Hill was treated during the 1991 Supreme Court nomination hearings for Clarence Thomas, yet he refused to directly apologize to Hill for the way he treated her. Here are some of the awkward questions he asked Hill while she was on the stand:[80]

> BIDEN: "Can you tell us how you felt at the time? Were you uncomfortable, were you embarrassed, did it not concern you? How did you feel about it?"

He also pushed Hill to say the name of a porn star whom Thomas allegedly alluded to.

> BIDEN: "Do you recall what it was?"
>
> HILL: "Yes, I do. The name that was referred to was Long Dong Silver."

Here is how his views about the hearings which he chaired evolved over the years.

October 1991—The Second Day of the Hearings

"I don't want to be a judge," he said.[81] "I hate this job. But all of my colleagues here are telling everybody how awful the process is. Let me be completely blunt about it: It's like democracy. It's a lousy form of government, except no one's figured out another way."

June 1992—Biden Blames the Republicans

"That's what makes me mad about the Republicans," Biden said at the time.[82] "What they do is they put you in a position on so many matters of principle that in order to fight with them and have a chance of winning, you have to either have the ability to go right above the issue, or you've got to do it the way they do it and disregard the rules."

2017

"Let's get something straight here, I believed Anita Hill. I voted against Clarence Thomas," Biden said in an interview with HuffPost.[83] "The only issue in the Anita Hill case was whether or not there could be information submitted in a record without a name attached to it, anonymously accusing someone of something," he said, referring to criticisms that he didn't encourage more women to testify against Thomas.

"The message I've delivered before is I am so sorry if she believes that," he said. "I am so sorry that she had to go through what she went through. Think of the courage that it took for her to come forward."

March 2019

"She faced a committee that didn't fully understand what the hell this was all about. To this day, I regret I couldn't give her the kind of hearing she deserved," he said at an event in New York City honoring students who helped fight sexual violence on college campuses.[84] "I wish I could have done something."

April 26, 2019

"I believed her from the very beginning, but I was chairman. She did not get a fair hearing. She did not get treated well. That's my responsibility," Biden said in an interview with *Good Morning America*.[85] "As the committee chairman, I take responsibility that she did not get treated well. I take responsibility for that."

Early 2020 Announcement?

Biden accidentally announced that he was running for president early in March 2019 at a Delaware fundraising dinner.[86]

"I have the most progressive record of anybody running for the United St—of anybody who would run," Biden said, quickly correcting himself as the crowd cheered.[87] "I didn't mean…" he added, his words trailing off into the distance.

Joe Biden Flip-Flopped on the Hyde Amendment

Until 2019, Biden supported the Hyde Amendment. Introduced in the 1970s, the Hyde Amendment bans the use of Medicaid dollars for abortion in all cases. In 1977, Biden voted against a compromise that allowed Medicaid to fund abortions with exceptions for victims of incest or rape or concerns about the life of the mother.[88] While the rape and incest exceptions passed, Biden voted again in 1981 to remove these exceptions.[89]

In his 2007 book, *Promises to Keep*, Biden describes his voting record on abortion as "middle of the road."[90] He wrote that he stands by Roe v. Wade, the 1973 Supreme Court decision legalizing abortion, and does not think he has "a right to impose my view on the rest of society."

Under immense pressure, Biden reversed his stance on the policy in June 2019.

Biden explained why he flipped on the subject during a forum for presidential candidates held by Planned Parenthood in Columbia, South Carolina.[91]

"I laid out a health care plan that's going to provide federally funded health care for all women and women who now are denied even Medicare in their home states," he said.[92] "It became really clear to me that although the Hyde Amendment was designed to try to split the difference here, to make sure women still had access, you can't have access if everyone's covered by a federal policy. That's why at the same time I announced that policy, I announced that I could no longer continue to abide by the Hyde Amendment. That's the reason."

Biden Flip-Flopped on China

Biden claimed in October 2019 that "China is not our problem," even though he once claimed China's rise as a country was a positive thing for America.[93]

Biden once scoffed on a trip to Iowa that China was a threat to the American worker.

"Come on, man.... They can't figure out how they are going to deal with the corruption that exists within the system," the former vice president continued.[94] "I mean, you know, they're not bad folks, folks. But guess what: they're not competition for us."

But he quickly changed his tone after Peter Schweizer, a senior political contributor to Breitbart News, wrote *Secret Empires: How the American Political Class Hides Corruption and Enriches Family and Friends.*[95] The book explained all about Biden's son Hunter's $1.5 billion deal with the state-owned Bank of China ten days after he visited the country with his father aboard Air Force Two.

"You bet I'm worried about China—if we keep following Trump's path," Biden said during a campaign swing through Iowa at the time.[96] "While Trump is tweeting, China is making massive investments in technologies of the future."

Biden Flip-Flopped on Gun Control

Biden got into a heated debate with an auto worker in Michigan about gun control, eventually telling the worker that he would not take away his guns.[97]

However, on a 2019 CNN broadcast, Biden supported a "national buyback program" for guns:[98]

> CNN: So, to gun owners out there who say, well, a Biden administration means they're going to come for my guns?

> BIDEN: Bingo. You're right if you have an assault weapon. The fact of the matter is, they should be illegal, period. Look, the Second Amendment doesn't say you can't restrict the kinds of weapons people can own. You can't buy a bazooka. You can't have a flame thrower.

> BIDEN: What I would do is—I would try to—I would institute a national buyback program and I would move it in the direction to making sure that that in fact is what we try to do, get them off the street.

> CNN: But that's not confiscating…

> BIDEN: No, that's not walking into their homes, knocking on their doors, going through their gun cabinet, et cetera.

> CNN: So people would be allowed to keep the weapons they already have?

BIDEN: Right now, there's no legal way that I'm aware that you could deny them the right to have purchased [ph]— legally purchase them.

"Nobody Should Be in Jail for a Nonviolent Crime"

Biden spoke about a radical change to the criminal justice system during the third Democratic primary debate in September 2019, bringing up the idea of ending prison sentences for nonviolent crimes.

"We're [sic] in a situation now where there are so many people who are in jail that shouldn't be in jail," Biden said.[99] "The whole model has to change, we should be talking about rehabilitation, nobody should be in jail for a non-violent crime."

However, Biden spent much of his Senate career advocating for "tough on crime" policies, especially when he authored the 1994 crime bill and went on national television in 1989 to push for the war on drugs.

In 1989, he went on national television to criticize then-president George H. W. Bush for not doing enough to escalate the war on drugs.

"Quite frankly, the president's plan is not tough enough, bold enough, or imaginative enough to meet the crisis at hand," he said.[100] He wanted not just harsher punishments for drug dealers but to "hold every drug user accountable." Bush's plan, Biden added, "doesn't include enough police officers to catch the violent thugs, not enough prosecutors to convict them, not enough judges to sentence them, and not enough prison cells to put them away for a long time"—a direct call for more incarceration.

He spent much of his time advocating for tougher prison sentences and increased funding for prisons in the 1994 Violent Crime Control and Law Enforcement Act.

When the 1994 crime law passed, Biden gloated that "the liberal wing of the Democratic Party" was for "60 new death penalties," "70 enhanced penalties," "100,000 cops," and "125,000 new state prison cells."[101]

"We Didn't Lock People Up in Cages; We Didn't Separate Families"

Biden falsely told the debate moderators during the third Democratic primary debate in September 2019 that the Obama administration did not "lock people up in cages" or "separate families."

"What Latinos should look at, comparing this president to the president we have is outrageous, number one. We didn't lock people up in cages," Biden told the moderator, before falsely claiming, "we didn't separate families."[102]

Meanwhile, Obama's Department of Homeland Security separated children at the border from their families and detained them in areas cordoned off by metal fences.[103]

Joe Biden Vowed Not to Use "Racial Wounds" for "Political Gain," Uses George Floyd's Dying Words in Fundraising Email

Biden claimed shortly after the death of George Floyd that he would not "fan the flames of hate," yet a recent fundraising email sent shortly after his remarks included George Floyd's dying words.[104]

The email read:

> "I can't breathe." "I can't breathe."
>
> George Floyd's last words. But they didn't die with him. They're still being heard. They're echoing across this nation.
>
> They speak to a nation where too often just the color of your skin puts your life at risk.

The email ended with a giant red button and the words *"DONATE TO ELECT JOE BIDEN."*

Biden claimed he also would not focus his speech on "fear and division," yet he spent much of that speech attacking President Donald Trump.

"The President held up the Bible at St. John's church yesterday. I just wish he opened it once in a while instead of brandishing it," Biden said, questioning Trump's Christianity.[105] "If he opened it, he could have learned something."

Later, Biden said, "I wish I could say hate began with Donald Trump and will end with him. It didn't and it won't."

"Donald Trump has turned this country into a battlefield driven by old resentments and fresh fears," Biden claimed, going on to say Trump's "narcissism has become more important than the nation's wellbeing that he leads."

Biden Claimed Women Should Be Given the Benefit of the Doubt, Yet Does Not Believe Tara Reade's Accusations

Biden denied that he sexually assaulted Senate aide Tara Reade back in the 1990s and said that her claim should be vetted, but when talking about Christine Blasey Ford, the woman who accused now-Supreme Court Justice Brett Kavanaugh of sexual misconduct, he said "women should be given the benefit of the doubt."[106]

Biden made the following remarks on NBC's *Today* on September 21, 2018, when anchor Craig Melvin asked about Ford's treatment in the Kavanaugh confirmation hearings:[107]

MELVIN: Dr. Ford has said now that she wants to testify, as you know, Mr. Vice President. But now the battle seems to be over how versus when. She wants to make sure that she's protected. She wants to make sure she's treated fairly. How would you suggest that the Senate handle these allegations?

BIDEN: I think they should do an FBI investigation. We did that for Anita Hill. It took two days, number one. And number two, most importantly, Anita Hill was vilified when she came forward by a lot of my colleagues, character assassination. I wish I could have done more to prevent those questions and the way they asked them. I hope my colleagues learned from that. Learned from that. She deserves to be treated with dignity. It takes enormous courage for a woman to come forward under the bright lights of million[s] of people watching her and relive something that happened to her, assert something happened to her. She should be treated with respect.

MELVIN: You brought up Anita Hill. You were chairman of the Judiciary Committee back in 1991. You were roundly criticized for not doing more during that hearing. Looking back on that, specifically, how would you advise senators to proceed next week? And how do you balance the rights of a woman who is making accusations like this versus the presumption that a person is innocent until proven guilty?

BIDEN: I think the presumption should exist, but what should happen **is the woman should be given the benefit of the doubt and not be abused again by the system.** My biggest regret was, I didn't know how I could shut you off if you were a senator and you were attacking Anita Hill's character. Under the Senate rules, I can't gavel you down and say you can't ask that question, although I tried. So, what happened was, she got victimized again during the process. I believed her when she came forward. I encouraged her to come forward. We were in a position where we got the FBI to do an investigation. And I voted against Clarence Thomas. He only got seven votes. He got seven yeses and seven noes; it was a tie vote in the committee. But I hope they understand what courage it takes for someone to come forward and relive what they believe happened to them, and let them state it. But treat her with respect. Ask tough questions. Ask substantive questions, "Where were you? What was said? When?" et cetera. But don't go after the character assassination.

Joe Biden Admitted He Was Never Arrested in South Africa Trying to Visit Nelson Mandela despite Claiming He Had Been

Appearing on a February 28, 2020, episode of CNN's *New Day*, Biden admitted that he was never arrested in South Africa on a congressional delegation trip to visit Nelson Mandela in the late 1970s:[108]

JOHN BERMAN: One thing that you've said repeatedly on the trail, I think it's three times now, you said during a visit to South Africa to visit Nelson Mandela, which I know was a very memorable visit for you, that you were arrested when you were there. Your campaign has since come out and said," [sic] No, no, no," you were separated from other people at the airport. But you didn't say that, but you did say "arrest" three times. Why?

BIDEN: What I meant to say was—look—I strongly, strongly, strongly, was opposed to apartheid. I was one of the leaders. If you doubt it, go on JoeBiden.com and look at the exchange between George [Shultz] and me on the foreign relations committee. And here's the deal, I was with a black delegation the Congressional Black Caucus, they had me get off a plane, the Afrikaners got on in their short pants and their guns, lead me off first and lead me in a direction totally different. I turned around and the entire black delegation was going another way. I said "I'm going through that door that says 'whites only,'" I'm going with them and they said, "You're not. You can't move, you can't go with them." They kept me there until finally it was clear that I wasn't going to move and what they finally did was they said, "Okay, they're not going to back the Congressional delegation go[ing] through the "black door," they're going to make me go through the "white door." They took us out—if my memory serves me—through a baggage claim area up to a restaurant, and they cleared out a restaurant.

BIDEN: **When I said arrested, I meant I was not able to, I was not able to move. Cops, Afrikaners, were not letting me go with them, made me stay where I was. I guess I wasn't arrested, I was stopped. I was not able to move where I wanted to go.**[109]

"Over 120 Million Dead from the Coronavirus"

Biden falsely claimed that the coronavirus killed 120 million people in a speech on health care in Lancaster, Pennsylvania, just moments before his livestream went dead.

"You have, unnecessarily, now we have over 120 million dead from COVID," Biden said, right as the live stream appeared to go under.[110] His image froze for about a minute before resuming at a different venue for prepared remarks.

This is not the first time Biden has flubbed the numbers on coronavirus. In May, he told MSNBC's *Morning Joe* that six hundred thousand Americans died from coronavirus when the data at that time showed the U.S. only had 65,068 fatalities.[111] The former vice president also forgot the name of the Ebola virus during that same interview and accused Trump of not having "intercourse" with the world.

"Over 600,000 dead, many of them who are those workers, those nurses, doctors, some of them," he said.[112]

"And we talk about that number like 600-plus thousand people," he said, before host Joe Scarborough interjected, "Sixty."

"Sixty thousand," Scarborough said.

"Six—sixty thousand," Biden responded. "I misp—60,000."

"We led—Barack Obama led on the corona, I mean, excuse me, in the pandemic that occurred when we were in office. It was kept in Africa," he told host Joe Scarborough.[113]

CHAPTER 3

MADE-UP STORIES

In this section, I've curated a selection of Biden's made-up stories that he has used throughout his public and private life, some starting as far back as when he was a college student in his twenties to made-up stories on the campaign trail and when he was finally elected as vice president of the United States.

Biden Bragged about Nearly Being Arrested for Chasing a "Lovely Group of Women" into an All-Female Dorm Room

Biden, who is now facing sexual assault allegations from a former Senate staffer, told voters during a campaign stop in Athens, Ohio, in October 2008 about a time he went to the city for a football game between the University of Delaware, his alma mater, and the local university, Ohio University.[114]

"Now I made a little mistake here that day, I made a little mistake," Biden told the crowd at the time, adding that after the game he "met this lovely group of Ohio University…students."

Biden proceeded to explain that he tried to convince two women he just met on campus to join him and a few friends at a local establishment.

"And uh, without knowing it, I shouldn't admit this on national television because it'll reveal that I'm over 60, but I thought that we were gonna go get something to eat," he said.

But the "two young women" first said they would "be right back," to which he offered to escort them back to their dorm rooms.

"I said well I'll come with you, and they said okay, and I walked into their dormitory and was immediately accosted by a cop who arrested me because back in those days men were not allowed in women's dormitories," Biden said.[115] "But I promise you I never breached the first floor and it was only a temporary detention."

The story made headlines because it was the first time Biden publicly talked about an arrest.

When Biden ran again for reelection in 2012, he clarified to voters that he wasn't arrested but he actually came close.

"The last time I was here, I want to make clear to the press, I didn't get arrested, but I almost did, because back in those days, you students won't appreciate this, men weren't allowed anywhere near a woman's dorm," Biden said.[116]

"And I got invited into a dorm. I thought I was walking into the waiting room; I got brought into the hallway," he said, laughing and adding, "I got escorted out very quickly by an Athens policeman."

Biden's Neil Kinnock Plagiarism Problem

Biden's penchant for plagiarism went beyond his law school days and into his campaign days when he was on the presidential campaign trail in 1987. That year, when someone showed him a political advertisement featuring then-UK Labour Party leader Neil Kinnock delivering a speech about working class backgrounds and progressive social policy, Biden was inspired and began to quote it while on the campaign trail.[117] However, his quoting turned into making it his own life story:

> KINNOCK: "Why am I the first Kinnock in a thousand generations to be able to get to university? Why is Glenys [his wife] the first woman in her family in a thousand generations to be able to get to university? Was it because all our predecessors were thick?"

> BIDEN: "I started thinking as I was coming over here, why is it that Joe Biden is the first in his family ever to go to a university? Why is it that my wife who is sitting out there in the audience is the first in her family to ever go to college? Is it because our fathers and mothers were not bright? Is it because I'm the first Biden in a thousand generations to get a college and a graduate degree that I was smarter than the rest?"

> KINNOCK: "Did they lack talent? Those people who could sing and play and recite and write poetry? Those people who could make wonderful beautiful things with their hands? Those people who could dream dreams, see visions? Why didn't they get it? Was it because they were weak? Those people who could work eight hours underground and then come up and play football? Weak?"

> BIDEN: "Those same people who read poetry and wrote poetry and taught me how to sing verse? Is it because they didn't work hard? My ancestors, who worked in the coal mines of Northeast Pennsylvania and would come up after 12 hours and play football for four hours?"

KINNOCK: "Does anybody really think that they didn't get
what we had because they didn't have the talent or
the strength or the endurance or the commitment? Of
course not. It was because there was no platform upon
which they could stand."

BIDEN: "No, it's not because they weren't as smart. It's not
because they didn't work as hard. It's because they
didn't have a platform upon which to stand."

Biden was not only plagiarizing Kinnock's speech; he was plagiarizing his life story. Kinnock's father was a Welsh coal miner while Biden grew up in Pennsylvania coal country, although none of his immediate ancestors were coal miners.[118] Unlike Kinnock, who was the first in his family to go to college, Biden had several family members on his mother's side who were college graduates. He also had a great-grandfather who was not only a college graduate but a state senator as well.

The whole scandal caused him to drop out of the presidential race in 1988.

"CornPop"

In 1962, Biden worked as a swimming pool lifeguard when he was approached by a tough guy by the name of "CornPop," or so Biden claims he was. In Biden's account of the story, CornPop was a "bad dude" who "ran a bunch of bad boys" as the leader of a Delaware gang called "the Romans.[119]

CornPop was reportedly threatening to "cut" the future vice president with a straight razor. But instead of calling the police,

Biden said he confronted the gang leader head on, arming himself with a six-foot chain.

CornPop allegedly backed down after a standoff.

Biden retold the anecdote in 2017 when he was rededicating a swimming pool and park in Wilmington, Delaware.

"CornPop was a bad dude and he ran a bunch of bad boys," he said.

Biden recalled one day that CornPop refused to wear a bathing cap, disobeying pool rules.

"You! Off the board, or I'll come up and drag you off," Biden shouted.

CornPop came down but was displeased, and said he would be waiting outside.

"He was waiting there with three guys [with] straight razors," Biden said.

"I walked out with the chain. I walked up to my car," Biden said. "I said: 'First of all…when I tell you to get off the board, you get off the board, and I'll kick you out again. But I shouldn't have called you Esther Williams, I apologize.'

"But I don't know if that apology is going to work."

"He said OK, closed the straight razor and my heart began to beat again," Biden said, noting that CornPop began to back down.

Even though there was no evidence that this story took place, then-Delaware NAACP president Richard 'Mouse' Smith bought into the same story.[120]

There was also a CNN reporter who tried to link an obituary for a Wilmington man named William L. "CornPop" Morris" who died at age 73 as the gang member in Biden's story.[121]

Biden Falsely Claimed He "Got Started Out of" an HBCU

Biden inaccurately claimed that he attended a historically black college or university at an October 2019 campaign town hall in South Carolina, where he was outlining his plans for education.

"I got started out of an HBCU, Delaware State, I don't want to hear anything negative about Delaware State here, okay," the former vice president said.[122] "But all kidding aside, the fact is that HBCUs are in trouble financially."

Biden instead attended the University of Delaware for his undergraduate studies, and went to Syracuse University College of Law to receive his law degree.

"Grandpa Finnegan"

At a 2012 reception for then-Irish prime minister Enda Kenny, Biden went through what he called a few made-up Irish sayings from his Grandpa Finnegan.

"My grandfather Finnegan, I think he made them up. But uh, it says, may the hinges of our friendship never go rusty," Biden said.[123] "Well, with these two folks that you're about to meet if you haven't already, there's no doubt about them staying oiled and lubricated here, ladies and gentlemen."

"Now for you who are not full Irish in this room, lubricated has a different meaning for us all," Biden continued.

Biden Made Up Emotional Story about the Afghanistan War

Joe Biden told a vivid tale to an audience of four hundred people packed into a college meeting hall in Hanover, New Hampshire, about how a four-star general asked the then-vice president to travel to the Kunar province in Afghanistan to recognize the "remarkable heroism" of a navy captain.[124]

"We can lose a vice president," he said. "We can't lose many more of these kids. Not a joke."

The navy captain, Biden said, rappelled down a sixty-foot ravine under fire, retrieving the body of a fellow American on his back. The general wanted Biden to pin a Silver Star on the captain despite the captain feeling like a failure.

"He said, 'Sir, I don't want the damn thing!'" Biden said,[125] his jaw clenched and his voice rising to a shout. "'Do not pin it on me, Sir! Please, Sir. Do not do that! He died. He died!'"

"This is the God's truth," Biden had said as he told the story. "My word as a Biden."

Only thing is, almost the entire story was made up. The *Washington Post* reported that Biden visited Kunar province as a senator, not as vice president, and that celebrated rescue was by a twenty-year-old army specialist, not a navy captain.[126] The soldier also never had a medal pinned on him by Biden.

CHAPTER 4

HUH?

This section contains most of Biden's jaw-dropping gaffes, ones that are hard to believe came out of his mouth. Most of these gaffes just speak for themselves.

"Wait—Your Mom's Still Alive"

At a St. Patrick's Day reception with then-Irish prime minister Brian Cowen back in 2010, Biden noted that his mother had passed away.

"His mom lived in Long Island for 10 years or so, God rest her soul, and, er, although she's, wait—your mom's still alive. It was your dad [who] passed. God bless her soul. I gotta get this straight," Biden said.[127]

"Stand Up"

During a 2008 campaign stop in Missouri, Biden asked the audience to give a round of applause for state Senator Chuck Graham.[128]

"Stand up, Chuck, let 'em see you," Biden said,[129] gesturing for Graham to stand.

Graham, who became a paraplegic in a car accident, was stuck in a wheelchair.

"Oh, God love ya, what am I talking about," Biden said, realizing his mistake. "I tell you what, you're making everybody else stand up though, pal. Thank you very, very much… You can tell I'm new."

Joe Biden: J-O-B-S Is a Three-Letter Word

During a 2008 campaign rally in the election against Republican challenger Sen. John McCain, Biden said "jobs" was a three-letter word.

"Look, John's last-minute economic plan does nothing to tackle the number one job facing the middle class, and it happens to be, as Barack says, a three-letter word: Jobs. J-O-B-S," he said.[130]

"Barack America"

In 2008 at a Springfield, Illinois, campaign rally, Biden was giving an introduction to presidential hopeful Barack Obama when he let his tongue slip.[131]

"This election year, the choice is clear," Biden said.[132] "One man stands to deliver change we desperately need. A man I'm proud to call my friend. A man who will be the next president of the United States—Barack America!"

FDR or Herbert Hoover?

Biden criticized George W. Bush's handling of the financial crisis during an interview with *CBS Evening News*.

"When the stock market crashed, Franklin D. Roosevelt got on the television and didn't just talk about the, you know, the princes of greed," Biden said.[133]

The problem is, FDR was not president when the stock market crashed in 1929, and television had not been invented yet. Biden's gaffe was picked up by the Associated Press and several other media organizations after the CBS News interview aired.

"Big F——ing Deal"

After then-president Obama signed Obamacare into law in 2010, Biden was caught on a hot mic at a press conference telling the president, "This is a big fucking deal."[134]

What's the Website Number?

In a February 2009 interview with CBS News, Biden was promoting Recovery.gov, a federal government website created for the American Recovery and Reinvestment Act. Problem is, he didn't remember the web address at first.

"You know, I don't know the website number, I don't have it in front of me and I'm embarrassed," Biden said.[135]

"30 Percent Chance We're Going to Get It Wrong"

When Biden met with House Democrats in 2009, the Democrats were facing criticism over the financial crisis and the $787 billion stimulus package that went along with it.[136] Instead of focusing on what the Democrats were doing right, he let out a Freudian slip and suggested they might be handling the financial crisis "wrong."

"Every once in a while, a generation of leaders gets a set of problems that are configured in a way that there's no historical precedent to look back on—other than our grit, other than some courage and determination—to know how to deal with it," Biden said.

"The president and I were talking about something yesterday in the Oval Office which, with the press here I'll not suggest what it was, but the response to the folks who were in the office was, if we do everything right, if we do it with absolute certainty, we stand up there and we make really tough decisions, **there's still a 30 percent chance we're going to get it wrong.**"[137]

"Beautiful Women"

Politico reported in 2009 that Biden was overheard commenting to then-Ukrainian president Viktor Yushchenko about women.[138] Yushchenko was talking about churches.

"I cannot believe that a French man visiting Kiev went back home and told his colleagues he discovered something and didn't say he discovered the most beautiful women in the world. That's my observation," Biden said.[139]

It was unclear which French man Biden was alluding to.

Biden Called Custard Shop Manager a "Smartass"

When Biden stopped at a Milwaukee, Wisconsin, custard shop in 2010, the manager told him the dessert would be on the house if he lowered taxes.[140]

"What do we owe you?" Biden is heard saying in footage captured by WISN-TV.

"Don't worry, it's on us," the manager replied. "Lower our taxes and we'll call it [the custard] even."

"Why don't you say something nice instead of being a smartass all the time?" Biden said a few minutes later.[141]

To put the cherry on top, Biden entered the custard shop mistakenly asking for ice cream instead of custard.

The Coronavirus Cure Will Make the Problem Worse

Biden appeared on an episode of *The View* in March 2020 when *View* co-host Sara Haines asked a question about whether businesses should reopen very soon.

"Are you at all concerned, as Trump said, that we cannot let the cure be worse than the problem itself?" Haines asked.

Biden said in reply **that the coronavirus cure "will make the problem worse, no matter what."**[142]

"Mr. President...Wake Up."

Biden criticized President Donald Trump during a June 2020 stump speech over his handling of the coronavirus pandemic, delivering a lethargic speech instead of what was supposed to be an amped-up call to action.

"I'm ready on day one. After more than three years in office, why isn't Donald Trump ready?" he said. "Mr. President...wake up. Get to work. There's so much more to be done."[143]

Biden then stared at the media for several moments before walking away, without taking questions.

Obama's Big Stick

In an April 2012 foreign policy speech, Biden applauded then-president Obama's approach to diplomacy.

"Now is the time to heed the timeless advice from Teddy Roosevelt: 'Speak softly and carry a big stick.' End of quote," Biden said.[144] "I promise you, the president has a big stick."

Joe Biden Brain Freeze: "The Rapidly Rising, Uh, Um, in with Uh, I Don't Know, Uh"

Biden struggled to read his notes placed in front of him at a brief appearance in Philadelphia where he participated in a discussion about reopening after the coronavirus pandemic.[145]

Biden seemed to lose his place while having a mask dangling from his ear.

"You know, the rapidly rising, uh, um, in with uh, I don't know, uh," Biden said.[146]

Joe Biden Badly Bungled Quoting the Declaration of Independence on the Campaign Trail

Biden badly botched a quote from the Declaration of Independence while at a campaign event in Texas back in March 2020.

"We hold these truths to be self-evident, all men and women are created by, go, you know, you know the thing," he said, struggling to remember the words of the widely known clause of the Declaration of Independence.[147]

"Super Thursday"

At that same March 2020 campaign event where he botched the Declaration of Independence, he asked voters to show up in a big way for him on "Super Thursday."

"Look. Tomorrow's Super Thursday," he said,[148] before correcting himself. "Tuesday," he continued as the crowd chuckled.

"I want to thank you all, I tell you what, I'm rushing ahead, aren't I?" he admitted.

What Office Did He Hold?

During an event with the NAACP in June 2020, Biden seemed to forget which elected office he first held.

"You've been with me for a long, long time—lifetime member. Got educated by the NAACP starting back in 1970 as a congressman, we were trying to—excuse me, as a councilman," Biden said.[149]

"I've Thought about What Would Happen If Trump Would Have to Leave Office"

Biden appeared on a June 10, 2020, episode of *The Daily Show with Trevor Noah*, and the two discussed what would happen if President Donald Trump had to leave office.

Trevor Noah started, "Let me ask you this, and I know this is a strange question to ask an American politician, may be easier around the world, but **have you ever considered what would happen if the election result came out as you being the winner and Trump refused to leave?**"

Biden replied, "Yes, I have."

After a pause, Biden stated, "I was so damn proud. You have four chiefs of staff coming out and ripping the skin off of Trump. And you have so many rank and file military personnel saying, whoa, we're not a military state. This is not who we are. I promise you, **I am absolutely convinced they will escort him from the White House with great dispatch.**"[150]

"10 to 15 Percent of Americans Are Not Very Good People"

Biden delivered a character analysis of some fifty million Americans by lamenting during an online event moderated by actor Don Cheadle that "there are probably anywhere from 10 to 15 percent of the people out there that are just not very good people."[151]

He also accused President Trump of dividing the country while pledging that he would be the one to unite the country and heal its wounds.

"The words a president says matter, so when a president stands up and divides people all the time, you're going to get the worst of us to come out," Biden said during the exchange.

"Do we really think this is as good as we can be as a nation? I don't think the vast majority of people think that," he continued. "There are probably anywhere from **10 to 15 percent of the people out there that are just not very good people,** but that's not who we are.[152] The vast majority of the people are decent, and we have to appeal to that and we have to unite people— bring them together. Bring them together."

Joe Biden Misstated Amount of Recovery Act Funds He Claimed He Oversaw While Serving as Vice President for Second Time in a Row

"Eight hundred and—I don't know, excuse me—it was 80— almost, uh, $89 billion—I guess it came to 84 at the end, 84 billion," Biden told Pennsylvania Gov. Tom Wolf during a virtual town hall event in May 2020.[153]

The week before, he misstated the amount of money he doled out during the Obama-era Recovery Act by $720 billion.

"I had the job of getting out $84 billion in 18 months in the Recovery Act," he said.[154]

The real number was $800 billion.

Biden Mixed Up Dates of D-Day and Delaware Independence Day in Same Breath

Biden was telling his supporters through a campaign town hall livestream that D-Day occurred on December 7.

"We declared our independence on December the 7th, by the way, you know, and it's not just D-Day," Biden said.[155]

D-Day, the day the U.S. invaded mainland Europe during World War II, was on June 6.

Delaware's independence day was wrong too. That day took place on June 15.

Democrats Need More People like Racist Democrat George Wallace

Biden once praised George Wallace, a notorious segregationist, and claimed to have received a reward from him.

"I think the Democratic Party could stand a liberal George Wallace—someone who's not afraid to stand up and offend people, someone who wouldn't pander but would say what the American people know in their gut is right," Biden told the *Philadelphia Inquirer* in 1975, referring to the then-racist Alabama governor.[156]

People in Jail "Can't Read"

Biden appeared on a May 2020 episode of *The Breakfast Club* radio show with Charlamagne tha God and suggested that people in jail have a few things in common, one of which is that they "can't read."[157]

"There's only a couple things everybody has in common in jail," Biden began. "One is they were the victims of abuse, or their kids were, or their […] mother was. Number two, can't read," he stated, offering no elaboration.[158]

"Number three, they don't have any job skills. They were in a position where they didn't get a chance," Biden continued.

"Why does it not make sense to have African-Americans who [are] getting out of prison who serve their time—everybody for that matter—be able to have public housing?" Biden asked.

"Politics Should Be the Most Honorable of Professions"

When he gave a 1973 speech before the City Club of Cleveland, Ohio, Biden was just thirty years old and had just won an upset victory to his Senate seat. He claimed politicians like him do better work than lawyers or doctors do.

"Politics should be the most honorable of professions," Biden said.[159] "Those of you who are doctors and lawyers and Indian chiefs in the audience, how can any of you possibly do as much good, if you are very good at what you do, as I can do if I am very good at what I can do."

"You can't," he added. "So the point is, this is where the action is."

"Football Analogy"

Also during that 1973 speech, Biden was attempting to illustrate to his audience how Nixon had to handicap Democrats ahead of the 1972 election by using football, but he blatantly said women wouldn't understand.

"The only analogy that I can really think of, is a football analogy," he said.[160] "And I apologize to you women in the audience for not being able to think of a more appropriate analogy, but they told me they didn't want you here anyway."

"I didn't expect any women to be here," Biden added.

"Corona-What?"

Biden seemed to forget the name of the coronavirus in an interview with Yahoo News.

"Thousands of meatpacker—workers got sick, got cona— uh, uh, got the virus and some died," he said.[161]

He forgot the name of the coronavirus again in a May 2020 interview with Al Sharpton on MSNBC.

"Everyone who, in fact, gets—is found to have the, uh, the, uh, the COVID, uh, 19 virus," he told host Al Sharpton.[162]

Biden also mixed up the H1N1 and Ebola viruses when talking about the coronavirus pandemic during his March 15, 2020, primary debate with Sen. Bernie Sanders (I-VT).

"We've been through this before with the coronavirus. Excuse me, we've been through this before with dealing with the viruses, the N1H1 virus as well as what happened with Africa," Biden said.[163]

Joe Biden: Coronavirus an "Incredible Opportunity" to "Transform" America

Biden vowed to "fundamentally transform" America in May 2020 by using the coronavirus to alter the country.

"And I truly think, if we do this right, we have an incredible opportunity to not just dig out of this crisis, but to fundamentally transform the country," Biden told a group of Latino supporters during a livestream.[164]

Biden has talked about using the coronavirus to advance progressive policies on several occasions.

On April 22, 2020, he said:[165]

> I believe, because, sort of, the blinders have been taken off, because of this COVID crisis, I think people are realizing, "My Lord. Look at what is possible. Look at the institutional changes we can make—without us becoming a 'socialist country,' or any of that malarkey—that we can make to provide the opportunities to change the institutional drawbacks..." from education, all the way through to all the other things we talked about.

On April 17, 2020:[166]

> We have an opportunity now to take, in a recovery act, a real recovery. We can fundamentally change the science relating to global warming.

"Intercourse"?

As I referenced earlier in the book, Biden appeared in a May 2020 interview with *Morning Joe* when he seemed to awkwardly phrase the word "intercourse."

"The pandemic is that the president has no intercourse whatsoever with the rest of the count—uh, the world," Biden said.[167]

He also confused the coronavirus with the 2014 Ebola virus, which was not a pandemic, according to the World Health Organization.[168]

"We led—Barack Obama led on the corona, I mean, excuse me, in the pandemic that occurred when we were in office. It was kept in Africa," Biden said.[169]

Earlier in the week, Biden said that travel bans prevent "economic intercourse around the world."[170]

Here is Biden's interview with CBS 4 Miami from April 28:

JIM DEFEDE: IF YOU'RE ELECTED PRESIDENT, WILL YOU RESTORE FUNDING TO THE WORLD HEALTH ORGANIZATION?

BIDEN: Yes, I will. But I will also insist that we do what we were doing before. We set up a pandemic office in the White House, President Obama. We had CDC, the folks for Centers of Disease Control stationed in other countries to anticipate when we might see a virus coming, a pandemic coming, because there's going to be more of these. I would be much more engaged in the world. We can't step back. If, in fact, for example, we solve the problem in the United States of America and you don't solve it in other parts of the world, you know what's going to happen. You're going to have travel bans, you're going to not be able to do, **have economic intercourse around the world.**

World War…9/11?

Biden staggered through an appearance on CNN alongside Dr. Sanjay Gupta and Anderson Cooper back in April 2020 where he muttered gibberish about a world war and forgot when 9/11 happened.

"Um, you know, there's a uh, during World War...Two, uh, you know, where Roosevelt came up with a thing that uh, you know, was totally different than a, than the, the, it's called, he's called it a, you know, the World War Two, he had the World, the War Production Board," Biden said.[171]

"You have [an] entire generation of young people beginning back in two-thou—when the attack occurred on 9/11 that in fact have been behind the 8-ball from the time they got out of school," he added.

"Luhan Province"?

Biden appeared on MSNBC back in March 2020 to talk about the coronavirus. Only problem is, he could not remember where it began.

"I insisted—I didn't insist—I suggested that we should have people in China at the outset of this event when it all started in Luhan province," Biden said.[172] "And what happened? We did not insist they go into the areas. That's all I can do—do what I know has to be done, so what I know has to be done."

The verbal flub came a week after he called the coronavirus the "Luhan virus" during a virtual town hall.[173]

Train of Thought

Biden held a virtual town hall in March 2020 with medical and emergency workers dealing with coronavirus and fumbled his way through his notes. He started out by touting President Donald Trump's stimulus bill, but his town hall went downhill from there.

"But there's a lot more. For example, you know, uh, um, I think there's more we're going to have to do as we go down the line here," he said.[174]

"For example, you know, uh, uh, additional checks to families should be, uh, um, um, should, conditions should [be] required, but I think there's a minimum, anyway, I won't go into all of that," he continued, giving up on the point.

"They Tell Me There's Ways They Can Do Teleconferencing"

During a press call, Biden said he was "desperately" looking to stay in contact with the American people and told reporters he had heard about this newfangled gizmo they call "teleconferencing."[175]

"They tell me there's ways we can do teleconferencing via us all being in different locations," Biden said.

"Iowa and Nevada Have Spoken" after New Hampshire Primary

Biden delivered a gaffe-ridden message shortly after he got blown away by the other candidates in the 2020 New Hampshire primary in February 2020.

"Tonight, we just heard from the first two of 50 states. Not all of [the] nation, not have…not a quarter of the nation, but two [states]," Biden said.[176] "Now, where I come from that's the opening bell. Not the closing bell."

He claimed that although "Iowa and Nevada have spoken," his campaign planned to contest the next series of primaries.

The gaffes, however, did not stop there.

Biden also claimed that his former running mate, former president Barack Obama, defeated an incumbent president in the 2008 election.

"All those Democrats that won against incumbents, from Jimmy Carter to a guy named Clinton and a guy named Obama, my good friend, guess what," Biden said.[177] "They had overwhelming African American support. Without it nobody's ever won."

Biden Claimed He Was Vice President in 1976

Biden made a stop on his bus tour in Iowa in December 2019 where he not only claimed he was vice president in 1976 but that he also created the Obama-era DACA program in that year as well.

"There's the Dreamers program, there's also a program that said we're not going to separate families, we're going to allow families to stay together while they go through the process, and the court said you can't," Biden said, before adding, "We did that in 1976."[178]

"And, I mean, I'm sorry, excuse me," the former vice president said immediately afterwards, seeming to catch himself. "Backing up here, 2014."

MLK, RFK Assassinated in the 1970s?

Biden was on the campaign trail in Iowa in August 2019 when he inaccurately claimed that Dr. Martin Luther King Jr. and Robert F. Kennedy had been assassinated in the 1970s. Both were assassinated in the late 1960s.

"Just like in my generation, when I got out of school, when Bobby Kennedy and Dr. King had been assassinated in the '70s—

the late '70s—I got engaged," Biden told the audience, before rambling about the counterculture movement of the 1960s.[179]

"Up to that time, remember, none of you women will remember this, but a couple men will remember it," he said. "That was the time in the early to late '60s, in the early '60s, the '60s, where it was, 'Drop out, go to Haight-Ashbury, don't get engaged, don't trust anyone over 30.'"

Biden Briefly Claimed He's in Ohio during Iowa Campaign Stop

Biden misspoke yet again at a campaign stop at Abby Finkenauer's fish fry in Cedar Rapids, Iowa, in November 2019, briefly claiming that he was in Ohio before stating his correct location.

"How many unsafe bridges you still have here in the state of Ohio?" he said before correcting himself.[180] "I mean Iowa. I was just in Ohio because they have more."

Biden to Auto Worker: "You're Full of S**t, Let's Take This Outside"

Biden got into an argument over guns with a Michigan auto plant worker in March 2020, specifically arguing over "AR-14s."[181]

The worker said, "You are actively trying to infringe our Second Amendment right to keep and bear arms."

Biden replied, "You're full of shit."

Upon further claims Biden was trying to take away the man's guns, Biden told the worker, "Don't tell me that," and suggested "going outside" to resolve the dispute.[182]

What Office Am I Running For?

When Biden was addressing the media in March 2020 in Philadelphia after another round of primary wins, the former vice president thanked his supporters before trailing off mid-sentence when saying what office he was running for.

"Our headquarters is just around the corner. And these are all people that have been working like the devil to try to get us elected as the uh…" he said before trailing off. "So I want to thank them," Biden said.[183]

The month before, he told an audience he was running for the United States Senate.

"You're the ones who sent Barack Obama the presidency. And I have a simple proposition here: I'm here to ask you for your help. Where I come from, you don't get far unless you ask. My name's Joe Biden. I'm a Democratic candidate for the United States Senate," he said.[184]

Biden continued, "Look me over. If you like what you see, help out. If not, vote for the other Biden. Give me a look though, okay?"

He never corrected his mistake.

Joe Biden Mixed Up His Wife Jill with His Sister

Biden confused his wife, Dr. Jill Biden, for his sister, Valerie, at a Super Tuesday event in Los Angeles, California, in March 2020.

Breitbart News reported that Biden took his wife's hand and introduced her to the crowd as his sister, saying, "[T]his is my little sister Valerie and I'm Jill's husband."[185] After he realized the two were on opposite sides, he acknowledged his flub.

"Oh no, they switched on me. This is my wife, this is my sister, they switched on me," he then explained.

Jaime Harrison for President?

Biden gave a victory speech after winning the South Carolina Democratic 2020 presidential primary in February 2020, endorsing Sen. Lindsey Graham's (R-SC) Democratic challenger for president.

"Folks, now we need to stand behind Jaime Harrison, the next president of the United…next senator," Biden said as he ended his campaign speech, referring to the Democratic Senate challenger to incumbent Sen. Lindsey Graham (R-SC).[186] He immediately corrected himself mid-sentence and continued his speech.

"DACA Illegals Are More American Than Most Americans"

Biden said during a campaign rally in Reno, Nevada, in February 2020 that DACA illegal aliens are "more American than most Americans are."

"Once again, **legalize all the DACA students**," Biden said.[187] "**These DACA students are more American than most Americans are**. No, I'm serious. Think about it. They come along when they're eight-years-old and their mom says they're crossing the…they don't know where they're from. They've never been [to their native country]. They've been good, decent citizens and they're great additions."

"Lying, Dog-Faced Pony Soldier"

Biden called out a twenty-one-year-old college student at a New Hampshire town hall event as a "lying, dog-faced pony soldier" after she questioned his electability.[188]

Madison Moore, a college student at Mercer University in Georgia, questioned Biden's electability after his campaign bombed in Iowa.

"You ever been to a caucus?" the former vice president responded. When Moore claimed she had, Biden said she had not. "No, you haven't. You're a lying, dog-faced pony soldier."

Angry Joe Biden: "Vote for Someone Else"

Biden was caught on cell phone video telling a Des Moines, Iowa, activist to "vote for someone else" during a heated exchange.[189]

Ed Fallon, a Democrat, was waiting in line to have his picture taken with the former vice president when they had the following exchange:

> Fallon started, "I'm going to support you if you win the nomination because we gotta get rid of Trump." He continued, "We got to stop building and replacing pipelines."
>
> Biden responded, "You have to go vote for someone else. If you're not going to vote for me in the primary."
>
> Fallon said, "I'm going to vote for you in the general if you treat me right."
>
> Biden said, "I'm not. I'm not. Look, you're asking for a picture with me and coming up and telling me you don't support me." He continued, "I'm looking at the primary and a caucus. That's what I'm looking for, OK? Now you believe that Bernie can do something by 2030?"
>
> Fallon said, "I'm actually supporting Tom Steyer."

Iraq, Iran, or Ukraine?

Biden mixed up Iraq, Iran, and Ukraine when discussing impeachment at a January 2020 town hall in Iowa.

He claimed that questions about his political influence crossing over with his son's work in Ukraine were part of an organized smear campaign against him. The claim, which U.S. and Ukrainian ethics watchdogs have disputed, was further undercut by the former vice president's inability to remember which country his son worked in.

"That's like just flat out acknowledging, 'We've been doing everything we do to keep Biden from being the nominee, and guess what: we tried it in Iraq, and it's not working....' I mean, in Iran. Excuse me. 'We tried it in Ukraine,'" Biden said.[190]

"We Should Unionize McDonald's"

Biden took a sharp left turn in his policy statements in December 2019, vowing to unionize the fast-food giant McDonald's if he were elected. The former vice president claimed it was vital to restore the power imbalances in the American economy.

"There is only one way you can fight back power," he said. "That is with more power, and that's union power...we should unionize McDonald's."[191]

Biden Called Voter "a Damn Liar," "Fat" in Response to Hunter Biden Question at Iowa Town Hall

At a December 2019 town hall in New Hampton, Iowa, a voter asked Biden a question about his son's Ukrainian business:[192]

> We all know Trump has been messing around
> in Ukraine over there holding their foreign aid

for them to come up saying they are going to investigate you. We all know about that.... But you, on the other hand, sent your son over there to get a job and work for a gas company that he had no experience with gas or nothing in order to get access for the president. So you are selling access to the president just like he was?

Biden said, "You're a damn liar, man. That's not true. And no one has ever said that."

The voter added, "I see it on the TV."

Biden said, "You see it on the TV. No, I know you do. And by the way, I'm not sedentary. I get up.... Let him go. Let him go. Look, the reason I'm running is because I've been around a long time, and I know more than most people know, and I can get things done. That's why I'm running. You want to check my shape on let's do push-ups together, let's run, let's do whatever you want to do number one. Number two no one has said my son did anything wrong, and I did not on any occasion—"

The voter said, "I didn't say you were doing anything wrong."

Biden said, "You said I set my son up to work at an oil company. Isn't that [what] you said? Get your words straight jack."

The voter said, "That's what I hear on MSNBC."

Biden said, "You don't hear that on MSNBC."

The voter said, "The hell I do."

Biden said, "Look, I'm not going to get in an argument with you."

The voter said, "I don't want to either."

Biden said, "Well yeah you do but look, fat, here's the deal—"

The voter added, "It looks like you don't have any more backbone than Trump does."

Biden Mocked Immigrant Activist: "You Should Vote for Trump"

Biden mocked an immigration activist at a campaign town hall in Greenwood, South Carolina, in November 2019 after the activist asked through a translator if he would commit to ending Obama-era deportations through executive action on his first day in office.[193]

"No, I will not stop all deportations," Biden responded. "I will prioritize deportations, only people who have committed a felony or a serious crime."

The activist, Carlos Rojas, began to lecture Biden about the deportations that took place during his vice presidency.

"You should vote for Trump," the former vice president cut off Rojas mid-sentence as the activist was laying out the Obama administration's record on immigration. "You should vote for Trump," Biden repeated mockingly.[194]

"No, I am not going to do that," Rojas responded, before demanding Biden pledge to end all deportations if elected president. "We want to hear you say that."

Biden Mocked "Classy" Reporter for Asking about Son's Love Child

Biden mocked a reporter in November 2019 for asking about his son Hunter's paternity test results. The results showed that Hunter fathered a child out of wedlock with an Arkansas woman.[195]

"No. That's a private matter," Biden snapped at Peter Doocy, a reporter for Fox News, when asked to comment. The former vice president then proceeded to mock Doocy for bringing up the subject.

"But only you would ask that, you're a good man. You're a good man. Classy," Biden said testily, in video captured by the *Washington Examiner*.[196]

"We Protect Geese Better Than Schoolkids"

During one of Biden's November 2019 campaign rallies in New Hampshire, he suggested that America protects geese better than schoolchildren.

"We protect geese more than we protect, no joke you can only have three shotgun shells when you go shooting for geese, we protect geese more than our kids," Biden said at a November 2019 rally in Concord, New Hampshire, where he addressed the issue of gun control.[197]

"Age Is Wisdom"

When the moderators during the October 2019 Democratic debates asked about how his age could affect his candidacy, Biden responded that it gave him "wisdom" to be president.

"One of the reasons I'm running is because of my age and my experience," he said.[198] "With it comes wisdom. We need someone to take office this time around who on day one can stand on the world stage, command the respect of world leaders."

Biden struggled throughout the night to demonstrate that his advanced age gave him an edge over his competition.

"Escalator"

Biden struggled to remember the word "escalator" when he was at a September 2019 campaign event in Miami, Florida, to commemorate the start of Hispanic Heritage Month.

"Remember when he came down, uh, down the uh—his golden escalator of Trump Tower," Biden said, according to video of the incident by the *Washington Examiner*.[199] "He announced on the way down, one of the reasons he was running was because of all those Mexican rapists."

Biden Falsely Claimed He Was Vice President during the Parkland, Florida, Shooting

Biden said he was vice president when the deadly Marjory Stoneman Douglas High School shooting took place. Only problem is, it happened in 2018, after he left office.

"[T]hose kids in Parkland came up to see me when I was vice president," he said.[200] But when they visited Capitol Hill to talk with members of Congress, lawmakers were "basically cowering, not wanting to see them. They did not want to face it on camera," Biden told a group of reporters in Iowa.

Margaret Thatcher or Theresa May?

Biden mixed up the name of former British prime minister Margaret Thatcher with former British prime minister Theresa May twice on the campaign trail. Thatcher left office in 1990.

He made his first gaffe at a fundraising gala in Columbia, South Carolina.

"Margaret Thatcher um, excuse me, Margaret Thatcher—Freudian slip," Biden said to growing laughter.[201] "But I knew her too." He then corrected himself, "The prime minister of Great Britain, Theresa May."

The second time he mixed the two up was when he delivered a speech to the Asian and Latino Coalition in Des Moines, Iowa, in August 2019.

"You had people like Margaret Thatch…excuse me," Biden said, catching himself.[202] "You had people like the former chairman and the leader of the party in Germany. You had Angela Merkel stand up and say how terrible it was. International leaders looked at us like, '[W]hat in God's name is happening to the United States of America?'"

"Congressman Biden"

Biden referred to himself as a "congressman," even though he never served in the House of Representatives. He spent his entire career in the Senate before becoming vice president.

"I've been involved from the beginning, as a young congressman—councilman, I introduced legislation to try to keep them from putting a sewer plan in a poor neighborhood," he told the debate moderators during the third 2020 primary debate.[203]

"President Bernie Sanders"

Biden accidentally called his Democratic rival Sen. Bernie Sanders (I-VT) "president" when attacking his Medicare for All plan during the third Democratic primary debate in September 2019.

"If you notice, nobody's yet said how much it's going to cost the taxpayer. I hear this, large savings, the president," Biden said of Sanders, before quickly correcting himself.[204] "My friend from Vermont thinks that the employer is going to give back if you negotiate as a union all these years, got a cut in wages because you got insurance."

"Record Players"

Biden was attempting to explain his proposal for eliminating the disparities for rich and poor kids in schools when he made a very dated reference to record players in his rambling response.

"Play the radio, make sure the television, excuse me, make sure you have the record player on at night. Make sure that kids hear words, a kid coming from a very poor school, a very poor background will hear four million words fewer spoken by the time we get there," Biden attempted to explain.[205]

Joe Biden Forgot Barack Obama
Was America's Last President

Biden forgot that his former running mate was the last president during a speech in New Hampshire in early September 2019.

"I'm the only guy that's beaten [the NRA] twice. I got assault weapons banned for ten years, it had to be reauthorized because of hanging chads in Florida," he said.[206] "The last president said no, I'm not going to reauthorize it."

HHS?

Biden seemed to forget the name of the Department of Health and Human Services (HHS) in an interview with an NBC affiliate in Iowa while he was discussing his proposal to expand Obamacare and lower drug prices.

"We should set up a system, which I've proposed [and] will if I'm elected president, that allows the folks at H-H, the folks at health and—the health department in the United States—HHS, to be able to go out and bring together experts and make a judgement when there is a patent being sought by a drug company," Biden said in an interview which aired in August 2019.[207]

"I'm Not Going Nuts"

Biden pushed back against his critics saying he is not fit for office by saying he is "not going nuts."

"I want to be clear; I'm not going nuts," the former vice president told an audience in New Hampshire in August 2019 after being unable to remember a speech he gave at Dartmouth College only hours prior.[208] "I'm not sure whether it was the medical school or where the hell I spoke. But it was on the campus."

Joe Biden: Putin "Coddles" Trump "like a Puppy"

Biden accused President Donald Trump of "coddling" Russian President Vladimir Putin, saying that the Russian president "carries" Trump around like a caged "puppy."

"While in fact, he's coddling Putin—Putin carries him around like a puppy in one of those little puppy cages," Biden said of Trump during a virtual campaign fundraiser with Sen. Tammy Duckworth (D-IL), who was in the running for Biden's vice-presidential pick.[209]

"I'm Joe Biden's Husband, Joe Biden"

Biden was about to give a speech at the National Education Association annual conference, and union president Lily Eskelsen García touted Dr. Jill Biden's membership in the organization before she introduced the presumptive 2020 Democratic nominee for president.

Biden, instead of mentioning his wife, mentioned himself.

"I'm Joe Biden's husband, Joe Biden," he said, not correcting himself and launching right into his speech.[210]

"Voter Registration Physicians"

Biden appeared on MSNBC's *The ReidOut* with Joy Reid in late July when he said his campaign would have lawyers going to "voter registration physicians" in the states once Election Day rolls around.

"We have a whole group of lawyers who are going out to every polling—every uh, voter, voter registration physician in the states—the secretaries of state, making sure that they, in fact, have a game plan as to how they're going to allow the voting to take place," Biden said.[211]

ENDNOTES

Chapter 1

1   Elise Viebeck, Matt Viser, and Colby Itkowitz, "Three More Women Accuse Biden of Unwanted Affection, Say Apology Video Doesn't Quell Concerns," *Washington Post*, April 4, 2019, accessed July 16, 2020, https://www.washingtonpost.com/politics/biden-says-hell-adjust-his-physical-behavior-as-three-more-women-come-forward/2019/04/03/94a2ed2c-5622-11e9-8ef3-fbd41a2ce4d5_story.html?noredirect=on.

2   E. J. Dionne Jr., "Biden Admits Plagiarism in School but Says It Was Not 'Malevolent,'" *New York Times*, September 18, 1987, accessed July 16, 2020, https://www.nytimes.com/1987/09/18/us/biden-admits-plagiarism-in-school-but-says-it-was-not-malevolent.html.

3   Haris Alic, "Joe Biden Refuses to Explain What He Meant by 'Roaches' in 2017 Video," Breitbart News, December 7, 2019, accessed July 16, 2020, https://www.breitbart.com/politics/2019/12/07/joe-biden-refuses-to-explain-what-he-meant-by-roaches-in-2017-video/.

4   Haris Alic, "Joe Biden: Japanese Women Are Only Employed Because of 'Xenophobia,'" Breitbart News, August 28, 2019, accessed July 16, 2020, https://www.breitbart.com/2020-

election/2019/08/28/joe-biden-japanese-women-are-only-employed-because-of-xenophobia-2/.

5 Alana Goodman, "Joe Biden Embraced Segregation in 1975, Claiming It Was a Matter of 'Black Pride,'" *Washington Examiner*, January 31, 2019, accessed July 16, 2020, https://www.washingtonexaminer.com/politics/joe-biden-embraced-segregation-in-1975-claiming-it-was-a-matter-of-black-pride.

6 Haris Alic, "1977: Joe Biden Worried Busing Would Lead to a 'Racial Jungle,'" Breitbart News, July 15, 2019, accessed July 16, 2020, https://www.breitbart.com/politics/2019/07/15/1977-joe-biden-worried-busing-would-lead-to-a-racial-jungle/.

7 Campbell Gibson and Kay Jung, "Population Division: Historical Census Statistics on Population Totals by Race, 1790 to 1990, and by Hispanic Origin, 1970 to 1990, for the United States, Regions, Divisions, and States" (Working Paper No. 56., Population Division, U.S. Census Bureau, Washington, D.C., September 2002), accessed July 16, 2020, https://mapmaker.rutgers.edu/REFERENCE/Hist_Pop_stats.pdf.

8 Ibid.

9 Shane Croucher, "Joe Biden's Biggest Gaffes: Quotes, Blunders That Could Hurt a 2020 Presidential Campaign," *Newsweek*, February 9, 2019, accessed July 16, 2020, https://www.newsweek.com/joe-biden-gaffes-quotes-2020-election-1323905.

10 Joel B. Pollak, "Pollak: Joe Biden's History of Division," Breitbart News, June 14, 2020, accessed July 16, 2020, https://www.breitbart.com/2020-election/2020/06/14/pollak-joe-biden-history-of-division/.

11 Candidate Research, "Joe Biden Praised a Racial Segregationist as 'a Man of Character and Courage,'" February 28, 2019, YouTube video, 0:19, accessed July 16, 2020, https://www.youtube.com/watch?v=9X6Y2CLqgDM &feature=emb_title.

12 Senator Joe Biden, "Sen. Joe Biden's Farewell Speech to the Senate" (speech, Washington, D.C., January 15, 2009), RealClearPolitics, accessed July 16, 2020, https://www. realclearpolitics.com/articles/2009/01/sen_joe_bidens_ farewell_speech.html.

13 Caitlin Byrd, "Joe Biden Attends Sullivan's Island SC Fundraiser Monday Morning," *Post and Courier*, September 16, 2019, accessed July 17, 2020, https://www.postandcourier. com/politics/joe-biden-attends-sullivan-s-island-sc-fundraiser-monday-morning/article_98618722-d8ac-11e9-96e3-f3c0070332cc.html.

14 Haris Alic, "Joe Biden Invokes Reformed Segregationist during South Carolina Fundraiser," Breitbart News, September 16, 2019, accessed July 17, 2020, https://www. breitbart.com/politics/2019/09/16/joe-biden-invokes-reformed-segregationist-during-south-carolina-fundraiser/.

15 Haris Alic, "Joe Biden, 1973: Full Audio Emerges of Rollicking Speech Senator Gave to Cleveland City Club," Breitbart News, June 7, 2019, accessed July 17, 2020, https:// www.breitbart.com/politics/2019/06/07/joe-biden-1973-full-audio-emerges-of-rollicking-speech-senator-gave-to-cleveland-city-club/.

16 Xuan Thai and Ted Barrett, "Biden's Description of Obama Draws Scrutiny," CNN Politics, February 9, 2007, accessed July 17, 2020, https://edition.cnn.com/2007/ POLITICS/01/31/biden.obama/.

17   Ibid.

18   Mario Trujillo, "Biden Refers to Asia as the Orient," *theHill*,
      September 17, 2014, accessed July 17, 2020, https://thehill.
      com/blogs/blog-briefing-room/218068-biden-refers-to-
      asia-as-the-orient.

19   Justin Sink, "Biden: 'Shylock' a 'Poor Choice of Words,'"
      theHill, September 17, 2014, accessed July 17, 2020. https://
      thehill.com/homenews/administration/217995-jewish-
      leader-slams-bidens-use-of-word-shylock.

20   Powerclam, "Joe Biden's Racist Slip," July 6, 2006, YouTube
      video, 0:33, accessed July 17, 2020, https://www.youtube.
      com/watch?v=sM19YOqs7hU&feature=emb_title.

21   Emma Kinery, "Joe Biden Says 'Poor Kids Are Just as Bright'
      as 'White Kids' at Event for Asian and Hispanic Voters,"
      Time, August 9, 2019, accessed July 17, 2020, https://time.
      com/5648481/joe-biden-poor-kids-white-kids/.

22   Rodney Hawkins, "Biden Tells African-American Audience
      GOP Ticket Would Put Them 'Back in Chains,'" CBS
      News, August 14, 2012, accessed July 17, 2020, https://www.
      cbsnews.com/news/biden-tells-african-american-audience-
      gop-ticket-would-put-them-back-in-chains/.

23   Ibid.

24   Joshua Caplan, "Brain Freeze: Joe Biden Says He'll 'Appoint'
      First Black Woman to the 'Senate,'" Breitbart News, February
      28, 2020, accessed July 17, 2020, https://www.breitbart.
      com/politics/2020/02/28/brain-freeze-joe-biden-says-hell-
      appoint-first-black-woman-to-the-senate/.

25   Charlie Spiering, "Joe Biden Claims 'I Come Out of the
      Black Community' during Democrat Debate," Breitbart
      News, November 20, 2019, accessed July 17, 2020, https://

www.breitbart.com/politics/2019/11/20/joe-biden-claims-came-out-black-community-during-democrat-debate/.

[26] Adam Nagourney and Jeff Zeleny, "Obama's Pick Adds Foreign Expertise to the Ticket," *New York Times*, August 23, 2008, accessed July 17, 2020, https://www.nytimes.com/2008/08/24/us/politics/24veep.html.

[27] Joshua Caplan, "Joe Biden: 'You Ain't Black' If You Don't Back Me over Trump," Breitbart News, May 22, 2020, accessed July 17, 2020, https://www.breitbart.com/2020-election/2020/05/22/joe-biden-you-aint-black-if-you-dont-back-me-over-trump/.

[28] Stephanie Toone, "Biden Says George Floyd's Death Has Had More Global Impact Than MLK's Assassination," *Atlanta Journal-Constitution*, June 12, 2020, accessed July 17, 2020, https://www.ajc.com/news/biden-says-george-floyd-death-has-had-more-global-impact-than-mlk-assassination/FZIrGKJBlDGFw2eqHCvCzH/.

[29] Katherine Rodriguez, "Alveda King: Joe Biden Playing 'Race Card' by Comparing MLK's Death to George Floyd's," Breitbart News, June 13, 2020, accessed July 17, 2020, https://www.breitbart.com/politics/2020/06/13/dr-alveda-king-joe-biden-playing-race-card-comparing-mlks-death-george-floyds/.

[30] Haris Alic, "Joe Biden Claims Trump Supporters Believe 'Mexicans Are Rapists,' 'All Muslims Are Bad,'" Breitbart News, April 16, 2020, accessed July 17, 2020, https://www.breitbart.com/politics/2020/04/16/joe-biden-claims-trump-supporters-believe-mexicans-are-rapists-all-muslims-are-bad/.

[31] Joel B. Pollak, "Joe Biden: If People Believe Tara Reade, They Probably Shouldn't Vote for Me," Breitbart News,

May 15, 2020, accessed July 17, 2020, https://www.breitbart. com/politics/2020/05/15/joe-biden-if-people-believe-tara-reade-they-probably-shouldnt-vote-for-me/.

[32] Lucy Flores, "An Awkward Kiss Changed How I Saw Joe Biden," The Cut, *New York Magazine*, March 29, 2019, accessed July 17, 2020, https://www.thecut.com/2019/03/ an-awkward-kiss-changed-how-i-saw-joe-biden.html.

[33] Sabrina Siddiqui, "'He Gave Me Permission': Joe Biden Jokes about Touching Complaints," *Guardian*, April 5, 2019, accessed July 17, 2020, https://www.theguardian.com/ us-news/2019/apr/05/joe-biden-touching-complaints-jokes-public-appearance.

[34] Croucher, "Joe Biden's Biggest Gaffes."

[35] Marina Fang, "Joe Biden Jokes about Inappropriately Touching Women—Again," HuffPost, June 4, 2019, accessed July 17, 2020, https://www.huffpost.com/entry/joe-biden-jokes-about-inappropriate-touching_n_5cf6a21fe4b0e8085 e41aa72.

[36] Colby Itkowitz and John Wagner, "Biden Says Trump Is America's First 'Racist' President," *Washington Post*, July 22, 2020, accessed July 23, 2020, https://www.washingtonpost. com/politics/biden-says-trump-is-americas-first-racist-president/2020/07/22/867017e8-cc4b-11ea-bc6a-6841b28d9093_story.html?fbclid=IwAR3gDQrgSv0Ss ZYtEE1xs3Q7amQKpcBHLXmiDEV9_P66v3JkF7I 39piEQ_4.

[37] Ibid.

[38] Dylan Matthews, "Woodrow Wilson Was Extremely Racist—Even by the Standards of His Time," Vox, November 20, 2015, accessed July 24, 2020, https://www.vox.com/

policy-and-politics/2015/11/20/9766896/woodrow-wilson-racist.

39 Amanda Seitz, "Joe Biden Was Quoting Racist Comments When He Used the N-Word in 1985," Associated Press, July 21, 2020, accessed July 23, 2020, https://apnews.com/afs:Content:9146840045.

40 Ibid.

Chapter 2

41 Arlette Saenz, "Joe Biden Believes He Is the 'Most Qualified Person in the Country to Be President,'" CNN Politics, December 4, 2018, accessed July 18, 2020, https://edition.cnn.com/2018/12/04/politics/joe-biden-most-qualified-person-president-2020/index.html.

42 Ibid.

43 Dionne Jr., "Biden Admits"

44 Ibid.

45 Ibid.

46 Ibid.

47 Matt Flegenheimer, "Biden's First Run for President Was a Calamity. Some Missteps Still Resonate," *New York Times*, June 3, 2019, accessed July 18, 2020, https://www.nytimes.com/2019/06/03/us/politics/biden-1988-presidential-campaign.html.

48 Matthew Boyle, "Joe Biden Lied in 1987 with Claim He Marched in the Civil Rights Movement," Breitbart News, June 3, 2019, accessed July 18, 2020, https://www.breitbart.com/politics/2019/06/03/joe-biden-lied-in-1987-with-claim-he-marched-in-civil-rights-movement/.

49 Robert Farley, "Biden's Record on Iraq War," FactCheck.org, a project of the Annenberg Public Policy Center, September

KATHERINE RODRIGUEZ

10, 2019, accessed July 18, 2020, https://www.factcheck.org/2019/09/bidens-record-on-iraq-war/.

50 Ibid.

51 Ibid.

52 Asma Khalid, "'Details Are Irrelevant': Biden Says Verbal Slip-Ups Don't Undermine His Judgement," September 3, 2019, in *The NPR Politics Podcast*, 23:25, accessed July 18, 2020, https://www.npr.org/transcripts/756872790.

53 Farley, "Biden's Record."

54 Tina Nguyen, "Here's a Video of Joe Biden Sounding a Lot like Trump," *Vanity Fair*, May 10, 2019, accessed July 20, 2020, https://www.vanityfair.com/news/2019/05/joe-biden-2006-vote-border-fence.

55 Marc Caputo, "Biden Blasts Trump's 'Racist Invective' in Immigration Plan Roll-Out," Politico, June 24, 2019, accessed July 20, 2020, https://www.politico.com/story/2019/06/24/joe-biden-trump-immigration-racist-1377518.

56 John Binder, "Joe Biden Uses Term 'Undocumented Alien' during Democrat Debate," Breitbart News, March 15, 2020, accessed July 20, 2020, https://www.breitbart.com/politics/2020/03/15/joe-biden-uses-term-undocumented-alien-during-democrat-debate/.

57 Binder, "Joe Biden."

58 Michael Barbaro, "A Scramble as Biden Backs Same-Sex Marriage," *New York Times*, May 6, 2012, accessed July 20, 2020, https://www.nytimes.com/2012/05/07/us/politics/biden-expresses-support-for-same-sex-marriages.html.

59 Edward-Isaac Dovere, "Book: WH Scrambled after Biden Gay Marriage Comments," Politico, April 16, 2014, accessed July 20, 2020, https://www.politico.com/story/2014/04/joe-biden-gay-marriage-white-house-response-105744.

60 Joel B. Pollak, "Joe Biden Did Not Sponsor or Co-Sponsor Any Juneteenth Bills in the Senate," Breitbart News, June 19, 2020, accessed July 20, 2020, https://www.breitbart.com/politics/2020/06/19/joe-biden-did-not-sponsor-co-sponsor-any-juneteenth-bills-in-senate/.

61 Ibid.

62 Joe Biden, "Juneteenth: A Reminder of Black America's Long-Fought Fight for Justice," *Essence*, June 19, 2020, accessed July 20, 2020, https://www.essence.com/feature/juneteenth-black-americas-fight-justice-joe-biden/.

63 Ibid.

64 Carol E. Lee and Amie Parnes, "Biden Says Avoid Planes, Subways; Puts Out Clarifying Statement," Politico, April 30, 2009, accessed July 20, 2020, https://www.politico.com/story/2009/04/biden-says-avoid-planes-subways-puts-out-clarifying-statement-021925.

65 John Hayward, "Fact Check: Joe Biden Claims He 'Saved Millions of Lives' from Ebola," Breitbart News, February 26, 2020, accessed July 21, 2020, https://www.breitbart.com/national-security/2020/02/26/fact-check-biden-claims-he-saved-millions-of-lives-from-ebola/.

66 Ibid.

67 Centers for Disease Control and Prevention (CDC), "2014–2016 Ebola Outbreak in West Africa," accessed July 21, 2020, https://www.cdc.gov/vhf/ebola/history/2014-2016-outbreak/index.html.

68 Joel B. Pollak, "Fact Check: Joe Biden Repeats False Claim about 'Shovel-Ready Jobs,'" Breitbart News, July 21, 2020, accessed July 21, 2020, https://www.breitbart.com/2020-election/2020/07/21/fact-check-joe-biden-repeats-false-claim-about-shovel-ready-jobs/.

69 Peter Baker, "Education of a President," *New York Times,* October 12, 2010, accessed July 21, 2020, https://www. nytimes.com/2010/10/17/magazine/17obama-t.html?_r= 3&ref=magazine&pagewanted=all%22.

70 ConservativeAlerts, "Obama: Shovel Ready Jobs Not Shovel Ready," June 14, 2011, YouTube video, 0:18, accessed July 21, 2020, https://www.youtube.com/watch?time_continue= 18&v=4p4-vPrcDBo&feature=emb_title.

71 Joshua Caplan, "Joe Biden Says He Worked on Paris Climate Deal with Long-Dead Chinese Leader," Breitbart News, February 25, 2020, accessed July 21, 2020, https:// www.breitbart.com/politics/2020/02/25/joe-biden-says-he-worked-on-paris-climate-deal-with-long-dead-chinese-leader/.

72 Joshua Caplan, "Brain Freeze: Joe Biden Says Son Beau Was 'Attorney General of the United States,'" Breitbart News, February 21, 2020, accessed July 21, 2020, https:// www.breitbart.com/politics/2020/02/21/joe-biden-falsely-claims-son-beau-was-us-attorney-general/.

73 Ibid.

74 Haris Alic, "Fact Check: Joe Biden Falsely Claims to Have Defeated ISIS," Breitbart News, January 14, 2020, accessed July 21, 2020, https://www.breitbart.com/2020-election/2020/01/14/fact-check-joe-biden-falsely-claims-to-have-defeated-isis/.

75 Ibid.

76 John Binder, "Fact Check: Joe Biden Falsely Claims Billionaire Donors 'Oppose Everything I've Ever Done," Breitbart News, December 19, 2019, accessed July 24, 2020, https://www.breitbart.com/politics/2019/12/19/fact-

check-joe-biden-falsely-claims-billionaire-donors-oppose-everything-ive-ever-done/.

77 Michela Tindera, "Here Are the Billionaires Backing Joe Biden's Presidential Campaign, as of September 2019," *Forbes*, December 7, 2019, accessed July 24, 2020, https://www.forbes.com/sites/michelatindera/2019/12/07/here-are-the-billionaires-backing-joe-bidens-presidential-campaign/#6a44d2b9159e.

78 Natasha Korecki, "Biden Says He Doesn't Need Obama's Endorsement," Politico, December 2, 2019, accessed July 24, 2020, https://www.politico.com/news/2019/12/02/biden-obama-endorsement-074856.

79 Ibid.

80 Croucher, "Joe Biden's Biggest Gaffes."

81 Matt Stevens, "What Joe Biden Has Said about Anita Hill over the Years," *New York Times*, April 30, 2019, accessed July 24, 2020, https://www.nytimes.com/2019/04/30/us/politics/joe-biden-anita-hill.html

82 Ibid.

83 Alanna Vagianos, "Joe Biden Says He's 'So Sorry' for What Anita Hill Went Through," HuffPost, November 13, 2017, accessed July 24, 2020, https://www.huffpost.com/entry/a-woman-just-asked-joe-biden-if-he-wouldve-handled-anita-hill-differently_n_5a09f7b1e4b0bc643a0d18f6.

84 Lisa Lerer, "Joe Biden Says He Regrets Role in Anita Hill Hearing," *New York Times*, March 26, 2019, accessed July 24, 2020, https://www.nytimes.com/2019/03/26/us/politics/biden-anita-hill.html

85 Stevens, "What Joe Biden Has Said."

86 Croucher, "Joe Biden's Biggest Gaffes."

87 ABC 10 News, "Biden Slips Hint at 2020 Presidential Run," March 17, 2019, YouTube video, 0:32, accessed July 24, 2020, https://www.youtube.com/watch?v=_P1hO2BoN e4&feature=emb_title.

88 Joe Biden to Delawareans, December 26, 1977, DocumentCloud, accessed July 24, 2020, https://www.documentcloud.org/documents/6127591-biden77letter.html.

89 Heidi Przybyla, "Joe Biden's Long Evolution on Abortion Rights Still Holds Surprises," NBC News, June 5, 2019, accessed July 24, 2020, https://www.nbcnews.com/politics/2020-election/biden-s-long-evolution-abortion-rights-still-holds-surprises-n1013846.

90 Ibid.

91 Li Zhou, "Joe Biden Explains Why He Flipped on the Hyde Amendment," Vox, June 22, 2019, accessed July 24, 2020, https://www.vox.com/2019/6/22/18713603/joe-biden-hyde-amendment.

92 Ibid.

93 Haris Alic, "Flip-Flop: Joe Biden Claims 'China Is Not Our Problem,'" Breitbart News, October 24, 2019, accessed July 25, 2020, https://www.breitbart.com/2020-election/2019/10/24/flip-flop-joe-biden-claims-china-not-problem-campaigning-iowa/.

94 Ibid.

95 Peter Schweizer, *Secret Empires: How the American Political Class Hides Corruption and Enriches Family and Friends* (New York: HarperCollins, 2018).

96 Charlie Spiering, "Floppy Joe Biden Switches Tracks on China," Breitbart News, June 11, 2019, accessed July 25, 2020, https://www.breitbart.com/politics/2019/06/11/floppy-joe-biden-switches-tracks-on-china/.

[97] AWR Hawkins, "Fact Check: Joe Biden Claims He's Not for Gun Confiscation," Breitbart News, March 10, 2020, accessed July 25, 2020, https://www.breitbart.com/politics/2020/03/10/fact-check-joe-biden-claims-hes-not-gun-confiscation/.

[98] John Nolte, "Nolte: Joe Biden's 'Buyback Program' Is Straight Up Gun Confiscation," Breitbart News, August 7, 2019, accessed July 25, 2020, https://www.breitbart.com/politics/2019/08/07/nolte-joe-bidens-buyback-program-straight-gun-confiscation/.

[99] Haris Alic, "Joe Biden: 'Nobody Should Be in Jail for a Non-Violent Crime,'" Breitbart News, September 12, 2019, accessed July 25, 2020, https://www.breitbart.com/2020-election/2019/09/12/joe-biden-no-body-should-be-in-jail-for-non-violent-crime/.

[100] German Lopez, "Joe Biden's Criminal Justice Reform Plan, Explained," Vox, July 23, 2019, accessed July 25, 2020, https://www.vox.com/policy-and-politics/2019/7/23/20706987/joe-biden-criminal-justice-reform-plan-mass-incarceration-war-on-drugs.

[101] Ibid.

[102] Joshua Caplan and Ezra Dulis, "Falling Apart: Joe Biden Delivers 9 Gaffes, Lies, and Awkward Moments in Third Primary Debate," Breitbart News, September 13, 2019, accessed July 25, 2020, https://www.breitbart.com/2020-election/2019/09/13/joe-biden-9-gaffes-lies-awkward-moments-in-third-primary-debate/.

[103] Charlie Spiering, "Donald Trump: Barack Obama 'Built the Cages' for Children Crossing the Border," Breitbart News, April 9, 2019, accessed July 25, 2020, https://www.breitbart.com/politics/2019/04/09/donald-trump-barack-obama-built-cages-children-crossing-border/.

104 Kyle Olson, "Joe Biden Vows Not to Use 'Racial Wounds' for 'Political Gain'—Then Includes George Floyd's Dying Words in Fundraising Appeal," Breitbart News, June 2, 2020, accessed July 25, 2020, https://www.breitbart.com/politics/2020/06/02/jjoe-biden-vows-not-to-use-racial-wounds-for-political-gain-then-includes-george-floyds-dying-words-in-fundraising-appeal/.

105 Ibid.

106 Penny Starr, "Flashback—Biden on Blasey Ford: Women Should Be Given 'Benefit of the Doubt,'" May 2, 2020, accessed July 25, 2020, https://www.breitbart.com/politics/2020/05/02/flashback-biden-on-blasey-ford-women-should-be-given-benefit-of-the-doubt/.

107 Ibid.

108 Joshua Caplan, "Joe Biden Admits He Was Never Arrested in South Africa," Breitbart News, February 28, 2020, accessed July 25, 2020, https://www.breitbart.com/2020-election/2020/02/28/joe-biden-admits-he-was-never-arrested-in-south-africa-i-was-stopped/.

109 Ibid.

110 Joshua Caplan, "Live Stream Freezes after Joe Biden Says 'over 120 Million Dead' from Coronavirus," Breitbart News, June 25, 2020, accessed July 25, 2020, https://www.breitbart.com/politics/2020/06/25/live-stream-freezes-after-joe-biden-says-over-120-million-dead-from-coronavirus/.

111 Kyle Olson, "Joe Biden Claims '600,000 Dead' from Coronavirus, Accuses Trump of Not Having 'Intercourse' with the World," Breitbart News, May 2, 2020, accessed July 25, 2020, https://www.breitbart.com/politics/2020/05/02/joe-biden-claims-600000-dead-from-coronavirus-accuses-trump-of-not-having-intercourse-with-world/.

¹¹² Ibid.

¹¹³ Ibid.

Chapter 3

¹¹⁴ Haris Alic, "Joe Biden Bragged about Nearly Being Arrested for Following 'Lovely' Women," Breitbart News, May 18, 2020, accessed July 25, 2020, https://www.breitbart.com/2020-election/2020/05/18/biden-bragged-about-nearly-being-arrested-for-following-lovely-women/.

¹¹⁵ Ibid.

¹¹⁶ Ibid.

¹¹⁷ Matthew Yglesias, "The Joe Biden Climate Plan Plagiarism 'Scandal,' Explained," Vox, June 5, 2019, accessed July 25, 2020, https://www.vox.com/policy-and-politics/2019/6/5/18653079/joe-biden-climate-plan-plagiarism-neil-kinnock.

¹¹⁸ Ibid.

¹¹⁹ Adam Gabbatt, "Why Is Everyone Talking about Biden Confronting a Man Named 'CornPop'?" *Guardian*, September 16, 2019, accessed July 25, 2020, https://www.theguardian.com/us-news/2019/sep/16/corn-pop-joe-biden-story-what-happened-is-it-real-swimming-pool-confrontation.

¹²⁰ WITN Channel 22, "Big Picture—Joseph R. Biden Jr. Aquatic Center—June 26, 2017," June 28, 2017, YouTube video, 38:50, accessed July 25, 2020, https://www.youtube.com/watch?v=SvCf1X2es0I.

¹²¹ Gabbatt, "Why Is Everyone."

¹²² Haris Alic, "Joe Biden Falsely Claims He 'Got Started Out' at a Historically Black University," Breitbart News, October 26, 2019, accessed July 25, 2020, https://www.breitbart.com/politics/2019/10/26/joe-biden-falsely-claims-he-got-started-out-of-a-historically-black-university/.

123 Paul Damon, "Biden: 'Lubricated Has a Different Meaning,'" March 21, 2012, YouTube video, 0:47, accessed July 25, 2020, https://www.youtube.com/watch?v=aRtP-PUQPPM&feature=emb_title.

124 Matt Viser and Greg Jaffe, "As He Campaigns for President, Joe Biden Tells a Moving but False War Story," *Washington Post*, August 29, 2019, accessed July 25, 2020, https://www.washingtonpost.com/politics/as-he-campaigns-for-president-joe-biden-tells-a-moving-but-false-war-story/2019/08/29/b5159676-c9aa-11e9-a1fe-ca46e8d573c0_story.html.

125 Ibid.

126 Ibid.

Chapter 4

127 Luke O'Neil, "'I Am a Gaffe Machine': A History of Joe Biden's Biggest Blunders," *Guardian*, April 25, 2019, accessed July 25, 2020, https://www.theguardian.com/us-news/2019/apr/25/joe-biden-2020-public-gaffes-mistakes-history.

128 Croucher, "Joe Biden's Biggest Gaffes."

129 Brad Belote, "Joe Biden Tells Chuck Graham to Stand Up," September 10, 2008, YouTube video, 0:40, accessed July 25, 2020, https://www.youtube.com/watch?v=C2mzbuRgnI4&feature=emb_title.

130 Urbanpanhandler, "Joe Biden 'J-O-B-S' Is a 3 Letter Word?" October 25, 2008, YouTube video, 0:18, accessed July 25, 2020, https://www.youtube.com/watch?v=BBHPvfAt5ow&feature=emb_title.

131 Croucher, "Joe Biden's Biggest Gaffes."

132 72390587192034, "Joe Biden: The Next President Is 'Barack AMERICA!'" August 23, 2008, YouTube video,

0:18, accessed July 26, 2020, https://www.youtube.com/watch?v=dKTjlAd-GXM&feature=emb_title.

[133] D'Angelo Gore, "Biden, FDR, and the Invention of Television," Factcheck.org, a project of the Annenberg Public Policy Center, September 24, 2008, accessed July 26, 2020, https://www.factcheck.org/2008/09/biden-fdr-and-the-invention-of-television/.

[134] FacebookDay, "Joe Biden to Obama: 'This Is a Big Fucking Deal,'" March 23, 2010, YouTube video, 0:49, accessed July 26, 2020, https://www.youtube.com/watch?v=HHKq9tt50O8&feature=emb_title.

[135] CBS, "Biden's Web Site Blunder," February 25, 2009, YouTube video, 0:34, accessed July 26, 2020, https://www.youtube.com/watch?v=nJnJKE8kkmM&feature=emb_title.

[136] Croucher, "Joe Biden's Biggest Gaffes."

[137] Jim Vicevich, "Fox News: Joe Biden 30% Chance of Getting It Wrong," February 6, 2009, YouTube video, 0:46, accessed July 26, 2020, https://www.youtube.com/watch?v=hCqqlYTi57A&feature=emb_title.

[138] Ben Smith, "VPOTUS, Overheard: 'Many Beautiful Women,'" Politico, July 21, 2009, accessed July 26, 2020, https://www.politico.com/blogs/ben-smith/2009/07/vpotus-overheard-many-beautiful-women-020042.

[139] Ibid.

[140] "Biden Calls Custard Shop Manager a 'Smartass' after Taxes Comment," Fox News, June 27, 2010, accessed July 26, 2020, https://www.foxnews.com/politics/biden-calls-custard-shop-manager-a-smartass-after-taxes-comment.

[141] Ibid.

[142] Bruce Haring, "Joe Biden Gaffe Alert: Stuns 'The View' by Claiming the Coronavirus Cure Will Make the Problem

Worse," Deadline, March 24, 2020, accessed July 26, 2020, https://deadline.com/2020/03/joe-biden-gaffe-alert-stuns-the-view-by-claiming-coronavirus-cure-will-make-the-problem-worse-1202891856/.

143 Kyle Olson, "Watch: Joe Biden Delivers Sluggish Finale for Stump Speech: 'Mr. President, Wake Up,'" Breitbart News, June 17, 2020, accessed July 26, 2020, https://www.breitbart.com/politics/2020/06/17/watch-joe-biden-delivers-sluggish-finale-for-stump-speech-mr-president-wake-up/.

144 CBS, "Biden Assures Voters Obama 'Has a Big Stick,'" April 26, 2012, YouTube video, 0:28, accessed July 26, 2020, https://www.youtube.com/watch?v=rrmbsKW0d7c&feature=emb_title.

145 Kyle Olson, "Watch: Joe Biden Trails Off Mid-Sentence, Fails to Read from Paper Statement," Breitbart News, June 11, 2020, accessed July 26, 2020, https://www.breitbart.com/politics/2020/06/11/watch-joe-biden-trails-off-mid-sentence-fails-to-read-from-paper-statement/.

146 Trump War Room, "Joe Biden Brain Freeze: 'The Rapidly Rising, Uh, Um, Uh, in with Uh, with Uh, I Don't Know, Uh,'" June 11, 2020, YouTube video, 0:10, accessed July 26, 2020, https://www.youtube.com/watch?v=e1b8Hpgkw4A.

147 Charlie Spiering, "Joe Biden Badly Bungles Declaration of Independence Quote in Stump Speech," Breitbart News, March 2, 2020, accessed July 26, 2020, https://www.breitbart.com/politics/2020/03/02/joe-biden-badly-bungles-declaration-of-independence-quote-in-stump-speech/.

148 Ibid.

149 Olson, "Watch: Joe Biden."

150 Ian Hanchett, "Biden: I've Thought about What Would Happen If Trump Refused to Leave Office," Breitbart News, June 10, 2020, accessed July 26, 2020, https://www.breitbart.

com/clips/2020/06/10/biden-ive-thought-about-what-would-happen-if-trump-refused-to-leave-office/.

[151] Simon Kent, "Joe Biden: '10 to 15 Percent' of Americans Are 'Not Very Good People,'" Breitbart News, June 5, 2020, accessed July 26, 2020, https://www.breitbart.com/politics/2020/06/05/joe-biden-10-to-15-percent-of-americans-are-not-very-good-people/.

[152] Ibid.

[153] Kyle Olson, "Joe Biden Again Misstates Amount of Recovery Act Funds He Claims He Oversaw," Breitbart News, May 27, 2020, accessed July 26, 2020, https://www.breitbart.com/politics/2020/05/27/joe-biden-again-misstates-amount-of-recovery-act-funds-he-claims-he-oversaw/.

[154] Ibid.

[155] Kyle Olson, "Brain Freeze: Joe Biden Misstates Dates of D-Day, Delaware Independence in Same Breath," Breitbart News, May 27, 2020, accessed July 26, 2020, https://www.breitbart.com/politics/2020/05/27/brain-freeze-joe-biden-misstates-dates-of-d-day-delaware-independence-in-same-breath/.

[156] Alana Goodman, "Joe Biden Once Said Democrats Needed 'a Liberal George Wallace,'" *Washington Examiner*, February 7, 2019, accessed July 26, 2020, https://www.washingtonexaminer.com/politics/joe-biden-once-said-democrats-needed-a-liberal-george-wallace.

[157] Hannah Bleau, "Joe Biden: One Thing People in Jail Have in Common, They 'Can't Read,'" Breitbart News, May 22, 2020, accessed July 26, 2020, https://www.breitbart.com/entertainment/2020/05/22/joe-biden-one-thing-people-in-jail-have-in-common-they-cant-read/.

[158] Ibid.

159 Haris Alic, "Joe Biden, 1973: Full Audio Emerges of Rollicking Speech Senator Gave to Cleveland City Club," Breitbart News, June 7, 2019, accessed July 26, 2020, https://www.breitbart.com/politics/2019/06/07/joe-biden-1973-full-audio-emerges-of-rollicking-speech-senator-gave-to-cleveland-city-club/.

160 Ibid.

161 Kyle Olson, "Joe Biden Forgets Word for Coronavirus, Claimed He Doled Out '$84 Billion' in Recovery Act," Breitbart News, May 20, 2020, accessed July 27, 2020, https://www.breitbart.com/politics/2020/05/20/jjoe-biden-forgets-word-for-coronavirus-claims-he-doled-out-84-billion-in-recovery-act/.

162 Kyle Olson, "Joe Biden Forgets Word for 'Coronavirus,' Loses Train of Thought," Breitbart News, May 2, 2020, accessed July 27, 2020, https://www.breitbart.com/politics/2020/05/02/joe-biden-forgets-word-for-coronavirus-loses-train-of-thought/.

163 Charlie Spiering, "Biden Fumbles Coronavirus Response, Mistakenly Refers to 'N1H1' Virus," Breitbart News, March 15, 2020, accessed July 27, 2020, https://www.breitbart.com/politics/2020/03/15/joe-biden-fumbles-coronavirus-response-n1h1-virus/.

164 Kyle Olson, "Joe Biden: Coronavirus an 'Incredible Opportunity' to 'Fundamentally Transform' America," Breitbart News, May 4, 2020, accessed July 27, 2020, https://www.breitbart.com/politics/2020/05/04/joe-biden-coronavirus-an-incredible-opportunity-to-fundamentally-transform-america/.

165 Joshua Caplan, "Joe Biden 'Excited': Coronavirus an Opportunity for 'Institutional Changes,'" Breitbart News,

April 22, 2020, accessed July 27, 2020, https://www.breitbart.com/politics/2020/04/22/joe-biden-excited-coronavirus-an-opportunity-for-institutional-changes/.

166 Charlie Spiering, "Joe Biden: Coronavirus Crisis an 'Opportunity' to Enact Green New Deal Policies," Breitbart News, April 17, 2020, accessed July 27, 2020, https://www.breitbart.com/politics/2020/04/17/joe-biden-coronavirus-crisis-an-opportunity-to-enact-green-new-deal-policies/.

167 Olson, "Joe Biden Claims."

168 World Health Organization, "WHO Director-General Briefs Media on Outcome of Ebola Emergency Committee," March 29, 2016, accessed July 28, 2020, https://www.who.int/en/news-room/detail/29-03-2016-who-director-general-briefs-media-on-outcome-of-ebola-emergency-committee.

169 Olson, "Joe Biden Claims."

170 Jim DeFede, "Joe Biden Confident He'll Turn Florida Blue, Says He'll Restore Obama-Era Cuba Policies in Exclusive CBS4 Interview," CBS4 Miami, April 27, 2020, accessed July 29, 2020, https://miami.cbslocal.com/2020/04/27/cbs4-joe-biden-interview.

171 Kyle Olson, "Watch: Joe Biden Stumbles Through Disastrous TV Appearances, Forgets Year of 9/11 Attack," Breitbart News, April 17, 2020, accessed July 29, 2020, https://www.breitbart.com/politics/2020/04/17/watch-joe-biden-stumbles-through-disastrous-tv-appearances-forgets-year-of-9-11-attack/.

172 Joshua Caplan, "Brain Freeze: Joe Biden Says Coronavirus Started in 'Luhan Province,'" Breitbart News, March 30, 2020, accessed July 29, 2020, https://www.breitbart.com/2020-election/2020/03/30/brain-freeze-joe-biden-says-coronavirus-started-in-luhan-province/.

[173] Kyle Olson, "Joe Biden Mistakenly Calls Coronavirus the 'Luhan Virus,'" Breitbart News, March 27, 2020, accessed July 29, 2020, https://www.breitbart.com/politics/2020/03/27/joe-biden-mistakenly-calls-coronavirus-the-luhan-virus/.

[174] Kyle Olson, "Joe Biden Struggles during Livestream: 'For Example, You Know, Uh, Uh…Anyway, I Won't Go Into All of That,'" Breitbart News, March 27, 2020, accessed July 29, 2020, https://www.breitbart.com/politics/2020/03/27/jjoe-biden-struggles-during-livestream-for-example-you-know-uh-uh-anyway-i-wont-go-into-all-of-that/.

[175] Kyle Olson, "Joe Biden: 'They Tell Me There's Ways We Can Do Teleconferencing,'" Breitbart News, March 20, 2020, accessed July 29, 2020, https://www.breitbart.com/2020-election/2020/03/20/joe-biden-they-tell-me-theres-ways-we-can-do-teleconferencing/.

[176] Haris Alic, "Joe Biden Delivers Gaffe-Ridden, Defiant Message after New Hampshire Blowout," Breitbart News, February 11, 2020, accessed July 29, 2020, https://www.breitbart.com/2020-election/2020/02/11/joe-biden-delivers-gaffe-ridden-defiant-message-after-new-hampshire-blowout/.

[177] Ibid.

[178] Haris Alic, "Gaffe: Joe Biden Claims He Was Vice President in 1976," Breitbart News, December 5, 2019, accessed July 29, 2020, https://www.breitbart.com/2020-election/2019/12/05/gaffe-joe-biden-claims-he-was-vice-president-in-1976/.

[179] Haris Alic, "Another Gaffe: Joe Biden Claims MLK, RFK Assassinated in the Late '70s," Breitbart News, August 21, 2019, https://www.breitbart.com/2020-election/2019/08/21/

another-gaffe-joe-biden-claims-mlk-rfk-assassinated-in-the-70s/.

[180] Hannah Bleau, "Gaffe-Prone Biden Briefly Claims He's in Ohio during Iowa Stop," Breitbart News, November 2, 2019, accessed July 29, 2020, https://www.breitbart.com/politics/2019/11/02/gaffe-prone-biden-briefly-claims-hes-in-ohio-during-iowa-stop/.

[181] AWR Hawkins, "WATCH: Joe Biden Loses It over Guns, Warns Worker He Will 'Go Outside,'" Breitbart News, March 10, 2020, accessed July 29, 2020, https://www.breitbart.com/politics/2020/03/10/watch-joe-biden-loses-it-over-guns-tells-worker-hes-full-of-sht/.

[182] Ibid.

[183] Kyle Olson, "WATCH: Joe Biden Trails Off in Victory Speech before Saying Which Office He's Running For," Breitbart News, March 11, 2020, accessed July 29, 2020, https://www.breitbart.com/2020-election/2020/03/11/watch-joe-biden-trails-off-in-victory-speech-before-saying-which-office-hes-running-for/.

[184] Ibid.

[185] Joshua Caplan, "Brain Freeze: Joe Biden Mixes Up Wife Jill with His Sister," Breitbart News, March 3, 2020, accessed July 29, 2020, https://www.breitbart.com/politics/2020/03/03/brain-freeze-joe-biden-mixes-up-wife-jill-with-his-sister/.

[186] Charlie Spiering, "Joe Biden Mistakenly Endorses Jaime Harrison for President in South Carolina Victory Speech," Breitbart News, February 29, 2020, accessed July 29, 2020, https://www.breitbart.com/politics/2020/02/29/joe-biden-mistakenly-endorses-jaime-harrison-for-president-in-south-carolina-victory-speech/.

187 John Binder, "Watch—Biden: DACA Illegal Aliens 'Are More American Than Most Americans,'" Breitbart News, February 17, 2020, accessed July 29, 2020, https://www.breitbart.com/politics/2020/02/17/watch-biden-daca-illegal-aliens-are-more-american-than-most-americans/.

188 Haris Alic, "College Student Felt Humiliated When Joe Biden Called Her a 'Lying Dog-Faced Pony Soldier,'" Breitbart News, February 10, 2020, accessed July 29, 2020, https://www.breitbart.com/politics/2020/02/10/college-student-felt-humiliated-when-joe-biden-called-her-lying-dog-faced-pony-soldier/.

189 KCCI, "Biden Tells Des Moines Activist 'Vote for Someone Else' in Tense Exchange," January 29, 2020, YouTube video, 1:41, accessed July 29, 2020, https://www.youtube.com/watch?v=2HHqcr43qr0&feature=emb_title.

190 Haris Alic, "Gaffe: Joe Biden Mixes Up Iraq, Iran, and Ukraine While Discussing Impeachment," Breitbart News, January 30, 2020, accessed July 29, 2020, https://www.breitbart.com/2020-election/2020/01/30/gaffe-joe-biden-mixes-up-iraq-iran-ukraine-discussing-impeachment/.

191 Haris Alic, "Joe Biden Goes Woke: 'We Should Unionize McDonald's,'" Breitbart News, December 20, 2019, accessed July 29, 2019, https://www.breitbart.com/2020-election/2019/12/20/joe-biden-goes-woke-we-should-unionize-mcdonalds/.

192 Pam Key, "Biden Calls Voter 'a Damn Liar,' 'Fat,' after Question about Hunter Biden," Breitbart News, December 5, 2019, accessed July 29, 2020, https://www.breitbart.com/clips/2019/12/05/biden-calls-voter-a-damn-liar-fat-after-a-question-about-hunter-biden/.

[193] Haris Alic, "Biden Mocks Immigrant Activist Asking about Obama-Era Deportations: 'You Should Vote for Trump,'" Breitbart News, November 22, 2019, accessed July 29, 2020, https://www.breitbart.com/2020-election/2019/11/22/biden-mocks-immigrant-activist-asking-about-obama-era-deportations-you-should-vote-trump/.

[194] Ibid.

[195] Haris Alic, "Joe Biden Mocks Reporter for Asking about Son's Love Child: 'Classy,'" Breitbart News, November 21, 2019, accessed July 30, 2020, https://www.breitbart.com/2020-election/2019/11/21/joe-biden-mocks-reporter-for-asking-about-sons-love-child-classy/.

[196] *Washington Examiner* (@dcexaminer), "@JoeBiden lashes out at a reporter who asked about his son's paternity test results," Twitter, November 21, 2019, accessed July 30, 2020, https://twitter.com/dcexaminer/status/1197624942227075072?ref_src=twsrc%5Etfw.

[197] AWR Hawkins, "Joe Biden on Gun Control: We Protect Geese Better Than School Kids," Breitbart News, November 11, 2019, accessed July 30, 2020, https://www.breitbart.com/politics/2019/11/11/joe-biden-on-gun-control-we-protect-geese-better-than-school-kids/.

[198] Charlie Spiering, "Gaffe Check: Seven Joe Biden Gaffes during the Fourth Democratic Debate," Breitbart News, October 15, 2019, accessed July 30, 2020, https://www.breitbart.com/politics/2019/10/15/gaffe-check-joe-biden-flubs-democrat-debategaffe-check-joe-biden-flubs-democrat-debate/.

[199] Carlin Becker, "Biden Struggles to Recall the Word 'Escalator' When Denouncing Trump's 2015 Rapists Comment," *Washington Examiner*, September 15, 2019, accessed July 30,

2020, https://www.washingtonexaminer.com/news/biden-struggles-to-recall-the-word-escalator-when-denouncing-trumps-2015-rapists-comment.

200 Emma Kinery, "Biden Misdates 2018 Parkland Shooting in His Latest Blunder," Bloomberg News, August 10, 2019, accessed July 30, 2020, https://www.bloomberg.com/news/articles/2019-08-10/biden-says-he-was-vice-president-during-the-parkland-shooting.

201 Simon Kent, "Sloppy Joe: Biden Confuses British PM Theresa May with Margaret Thatcher (Who Left Office in 1990)," Breitbart News, May 6, 2019, accessed July 30, 2020, https://www.breitbart.com/politics/2019/05/06/sloppy-joe-biden-confuses-british-pm-theresa-may-with-margaret-thatcher-who-left-office-in-1990/.

202 Haris Alic, "Another Gaffe: Joe Biden Mixes Up Iowa and Vermont at First Event after Lengthy Rest," Breitbart News, August 17, 2019, accessed July 30, 2020, https://www.breitbart.com/2020-election/2019/08/17/another-gaffe-joe-biden-mixes-up-iowa-and-vermont-at-first-event-after-lengthy-rest/.

203 Joshua Caplan and Ezra Dulis, "Falling Apart: Joe Biden Delivers 9 Gaffes, Lies, and Awkward Moments in Third Primary Debate," Breitbart News, September 13, 2019, accessed July 30, 2020, https://www.breitbart.com/2020-election/2019/09/13/joe-biden-9-gaffes-lies-awkward-moments-in-third-primary-debate/.

204 Haris Alic, "Democrat Debate: Joe Biden Refers to Bernie Sanders as 'The President,'" Breitbart News, September 12, 2019, accessed July 30, 2020, https://www.breitbart.com/2020-election/2019/09/12/democrat-debate-joe-biden-refers-bernie-sanders-president/

[205] Caplan and Dulis, "Falling Apart."

[206] Haris Alic, "Joe Biden Forgets Barack Obama Was America's 'Last President' in Latest Gaffe," Breitbart News, September 7, 2019, accessed July 30, 2020, https://www.breitbart.com/2020-election/2019/09/07/joe-biden-forgets-barack-obama-was-americas-last-president-in-latest-lapse/.

[207] Haris Alic, "Joe Biden Struggles to Remember HHS When Discussing Healthcare," Breitbart News, August 27, 2019, accessed July 30, 2020, https://www.breitbart.com/2020-election/2019/08/27/jjoe-biden-struggles-to-remember-hhs-when-discussing-healthcare/.

[208] Haris Alic, "Joe Biden Pushes Back at Detractors over Gaffes: 'I'm Not Going Nuts,'" Breitbart News, August 26, 2019, accessed July 30, 2020, https://www.breitbart.com/2020-election/2019/08/26/joe-biden-pushes-back-detractors-gaffes-not-going-nuts/.

[209] Joshua Caplan, "Joe Biden: Putin Carries Trump Around Like a Puppy," Breitbart News, July 7, 2020, accessed July 30, 2020, https://www.breitbart.com/2020-election/2020/07/07/joe-biden-putin-carries-trump-puppy/.

[210] Kyle Olson, "Joe Biden: 'I'm Joe Biden's Husband, Joe Biden,'" Breitbart News, July 3, 2020, accessed July 30, 2020, https://www.breitbart.com/politics/2020/07/03/joe-bidens-husband-joe-biden/.

[211] Kyle Olson, "Joe Biden: We Have Lawyers Going Out to Every Polling, Every Uh, Voter Registration Physician in the States," Breitbart News, July 21, 2020, accessed July 30, 2020, https://www.breitbart.com/politics/2020/07/21/joe-biden-we-have-lawyers-going-out-to-every-polling-every-uh-voter-registration-physician-in-the-states/.

ACKNOWLEDGMENTS

I would like to thank my publisher, David Bernstein, for all his hard work in helping me get this book to print.

I would also like to thank Heather King, for assisting in the publishing process.

I would also like to thank my mentor, Wynton Hall, for giving me the sage advice I needed to write this book. I will be forever grateful for your advice.

I would also like to thank my family for always being there for me no matter what.

ABOUT THE AUTHOR

Photo by America's Future Foundation

Katherine Rodriguez is a reporter for Breitbart News who covers trending issues on topics in politics, crime, entertainment, health, and more. In 2014, she graduated from George Washington University with a bachelor's degree in journalism.

Made in the USA
Coppell, TX
29 September 2020

38974693R00066